"*Houle makes a great case that this new decade will have major disruptions that will affect us all. He lists the Age of Intelligence, the Age of Climate Change and the clear coming reality that both Capitalism and Democracy must be reinvented during the 2020s. I recommend this book to anyone who wants to be ready and prepared for what is ahead.*"
Bill Johnston, Former President of the NYSE, and concerned grandfather

"*Houle is one of my favorite futurists. Take this provocative tour of this decade's boiling issues and hot solutions.*"
Philip Kotler, S.C.Johnson & Son Distinguished Professor of International Marketing, Northwestern University, Kellogg School of Management

"*In this first of a projected series of books about the 2020s, David Houle sets the stage for what looks to be a decade of unprecedented change. A short and fast read this book should be considered as a guidebook for this new decade. Highly recommended!*"
James E. Duffy, Former President of the ABC Television Network, Former spokesperson for the Barbara Bush Literacy Foundation

"*David Houle is at the top of his game with this book. I first heard him deliver a keynote last summer and had my mind opened up in a way that rarely happens at conferences. In this book he clearly lays out, in 10 short chapters, all the big trends that will shape this new decade. A guidebook for the future that I highly recommend.*"
Dr. Ivan Misner, NY Times Bestselling Author and Founder of BNI

"As we face unprecedented times at the start of this decade and the acceleration of technology continues its blistering pace, I worry for humanity that we are unprepared and lacking true leadership to meet the challenges before us. Step 1 is to understand and get context to where we truly stand, what we are dealing with and what the trend lines show and what that means for us individually and collectively. David Houle helps us gain this understanding better than anyone, through thought provoking, insightful and research-backed analysis. This first installment of 'The 2020s' series is mind blowing yet very matter of fact.

What is most appealing is that David doesn't focus exclusively on information and problems, but provides digestible explanations as well as hopeful and practical prescriptions for humanity that anyone, including common citizens, organizations and government leaders, can implement. To confidently 'Face the Future' as David articulates, the concepts and recommendations from this book ought to be in every crew member's arsenal. I have been fortunate enough to be a direct beneficiary of David's wisdom, as he has mentored me directly for two decades now."
Arman Rousta, Founder of b.labs Ventures and The Polymath Project

"I have known David for more than 10 years. During that entire time, he has been spot-on in his forecasts about the major events and trends that will happen. As the CEO of a leading health care organization, David always delivers information that gives us a competitive advantage. This book is an introduction for all of us about the next ten years. We all need to get ready and be prepared. This book is a must read." Jonathan Fleece, President & CEO, Stratum Health Systems and Tidewell Hospice

THE 2020S:
The Most Disruptive Decade In History

David Houle

Dedication

To Victoria with love and gratitude. Thank you for the experience of facing COVID-19 together, your 15 years of disaster help with the Red Cross was essential. Thank you for understanding that books always seem to take longer than expected.

To Christopher, wherever you are living in the world, the 2020s will greatly shape you for the rest of your life. Be open, adaptive and resilient and you will do well. Thank you for being such a great son.

To Jordan, may the 2020s provide you with ample opportunities to succeed. Be fully open to the new as that is what will define this decade. Adapt and thrive. Thank you for being such a great stepson.

To all those visionaries and forward thinkers who have long seen that our immediate collective future can be a transcendent one if we let go of the limitations from the past.

Table of Contents

Acknowledgements

First I want to thank Bob Leonard, the editor of this book. Bob is a talented editor and a patient one. He co-authored "Moving to a Finite Earth Economy – Crew Manual" with me. We have worked together on articles, books, blogs and columns that we feel are essential reading for those concerned with our climate crisis, the need to reinvent capitalism, and the transformative possibility of a new and emerging consciousness. Know you are valued.

Dave Abrahamsen and his design firm What2Design has been my creative support for the last 14 years. He has designed, built and maintained all my web sites, designed the covers of my books (including this one) and makes me look good to the world. I always excitedly anticipate his designs and visual ideas.

I want to thank my colleagues at The Sarasota Institute – a 21stCentury Think Tank for their support and intellectual stimulation. Particularly Jason Voss, Phil Kotler, Carol Probstfeld, Lucie Lapovsky and Becky Van de Bogert who stood up at a most critical time with intellectual fire power and support for the launch of the Institute. Karen Holbrook and Don O'Shea gave me institutional and intellectual support when needed.

I want to thank all the great creative minds at the Ringling College of Art + Design, where I am Futurist in Residence – particularly Larry Thompson, Doug Chismar and Tim Rumage. Larry is a true force of nature and the reason that

Ringling College is now one of the top art and design colleges in the world. Doug showed me the limits of my knowledge with kind suggestions and recommendations. Tim taught me more about the environment and our climate crisis than anyone else, and is the only planetary ethicist I know.

Thanks to Bill Johnston, a good friend and my own wise elder. Bill has given great advice and provided essential support to my efforts to change the world for the better.

Jonathan Fleece is a great friend, a co-author, and an inspirational leader in the world of Hospice. Jonathan and I are together ahead of the curve in many areas of healthcare in America.

Thanks to Cliff Walters, who I view as a wise elder, even though we are the same age. Whenever I have a conversation with Cliff, I am always wiser for it.

Thanks to Mike Shatzkin, a great friend and a fellow aging boomer (which is a bond in and of itself). Mike has forgotten more about the world of publishing than most people ever learn, and has thus been my publishing guru. He is rarely at a loss for words, which is good because so much of what he says is insightful.

Then of course are all the intellectual, visionary, spiritual and inspirational authors and creators who have shaped who I am and who are a part of this book. Alvin Toffler, Marshall McLuhan, R. Buckminster Fuller, Teilhard de Jardin, Bob Dylan, the Rolling Stones, Led Zeppelin, Isaac Asimov, Robert Heinlein, Frank Herbert, Bruce Lee, Bobby Kennedy, Ram Dass, the Dalai Lama, Jack Kerouac, Henry Miller, Ernest Hemingway, John D. McDonald, Miles Davis and innumerable blues artists whose names would double the length of this paragraph.

I am sure I have forgotten some names that should be here, and I apologize directly to you. Sometimes, my memory may falter, but my vision of the future remains clear.

Quotes

"We should try to be the parents of our future rather than the offspring of our past."

Miguel de Unamuno (1864 –1936), Spanish essayist, novelist, poet, playwright, and Philosopher

"In the revelation of the truth there are three stages. In the first it is ridiculed. In the second it is resisted. In the third it is considered self-evident."

Arthur Schopenhauer (1778 – 1860), German Philosopher

"The illiterate of the 21st century will not be those that cannot read or write. It will be those that cannot learn, unlearn and relearn."

Alvin Toffler (1928 – 2016), American Futurist

"Don't get set into one form, adapt it and build your own, and let it grow, be like water. Empty your mind: be formless, shapeless like water. You put water in a cup, it becomes the cup; you put water into a bottle it becomes the bottle; you put it in a teapot it becomes the teapot. Be water, my friend."

Bruce Lee (1940 – 1973), American martial artist and actor

Prologue

As the final draft of this book was being written, COVID-19 was spreading around the world. In late March 2020, we are looking at a global pandemic, lack of global governmental systems thinking, fear and uncertainty and our first fork in the road socially, culturally and economically. The long term non-medical consequences post COVID-19 will be significant, depending on how long the pandemic is front and center in our lives.

So, 90 days into the 2020s we are getting a taste of why it will be the most disruptive and transformative decade in our history. In a period of months there has been a financial market collapse, hundreds of thousands of cases of COVID-19, government failure to lead, and ever more reliance on technology and social separation. The financial markets are confronted with realities not experienced since the Great Depression. Health systems are showing their glaring flaws. Social interaction is being fully disrupted. Trillions of dollars will be spent to shore up existing systems and economies.

This is one of many coming disruptions, where the growing interconnectedness of humanity will mean that a crisis in one area of life will affect many other aspects of our society and culture. Upheavals with ever increasing, cascading effects across human endeavor.

It is not Armageddon, though our 20th century wired brains and older religious roots will tell us that it might be. It will be up to us to transcend our old ways of thinking, and reference points from the past, to fully face the future. We have the potential to find our way to the future, the path to happiness and abundance, but we must understand that almost everything will change.

As of this writing we are three months or 1/40 of the way through the 2020s, suggesting that disruption, transformation and our rough trajectory going forward will be of massive importance. Please think of this book and the ones that will follow as travel guides to our future and our next evolutionary step.

March 2020

Introduction

The 2020s will be the most disruptive and transformative decade in history. There is no major part of society, culture, business, economics, politics or civilization that will not be disrupted and changed in the next ten years. In fact, it is these next ten years that will set the direction of civilization for the rest of the century.

This is the first book of a series that will examine the big trends, forces, changes and disruptions of this decade. This book provides an overview and a call to awareness to prepare... as prepare we must. There is no turning back, no wishing fondly for what we thought reality was, as massive change is upon us.

On many fundamental levels, we are entering the conclusion of the Shift Age, which will be looked back upon as the transition from the historical reality humanity has experienced up to 2000 to the new, altered reality we will be living in by the 2030s.

For those of you who know my work, read my books, blogs, columns or heard me speak in person, thank you for returning. For those of you who are reading a book of mine for the first time, here is a brief introduction. After living a life that, in many cases, was "ahead of the curve"[1], I became a full-time futurist in 2005. As a young man I read many science fiction novels and non-fiction books written by futurists. The three most influential futurists of the 20th century – R. Buckminster Fuller, Marshall McLuhan and Alvin Toffler – shaped my thinking… and still do so to this day. I stand on the shoulders of these three great visionaries to see further into the 21st century than they could. The clarity of thought and just the enormity of the intellects of these three men are still of great value in navigating our future.

As we have learned in the last 50 years, science fiction often becomes science fact. This will accelerate in the 2020s. Hand-held devices, body scanners, brain implants, space travel, driverless vehicles, a dramatically changed definition of the workplace, entirely new business models, life expectancy extension beyond 100, genetic enhancement and, especially, an evolving collective consciousness across humanity will significantly impact 2020s. Fiction becomes fact. Imagination becomes manifest in the real world.

We stand at the apotheosis of human evolution. We are smarter, bigger, more technologically integrated, wealthier and better educated than at any time in history. In the last two centuries, the Industrial Age and then the Information Age delivered the greatest amount of financial wealth, scientific discoveries, health improvements and educational upgrades than ever before.

[1] https://davidhoule.com/bio

Standing at this historical peak of human accomplishment, we have a true chance to take our next evolutionary leap. We can successfully navigate the dynamics rushing toward us to realize a merging of humanity and technology. That integration can springboard us to an unprecedented era of abundance, higher consciousness and a global inter-connectedness.

However, the 2020s could also be a time of reckoning, because we are at a fork in the road on many levels. Across the board we will be facing decisions as a species that will determine the path of human civilization for the rest of this century and beyond.

The coming decade will shape the future in ways almost unimaginable.

Let's take a look!

Chapter 1 The Shift Age - A Time of Transition

We are in the Shift Age. It is the transitional time between what was our collective reality up to the year 2000 and what will be our new reality by the 2030s. Ages never start at any specific time, but usually transition into the new reality over a decade or less. To pick specific start dates or years is specious. That said, I suggested that the Shift Age had begun around 2005, mid-decade. I think it will deliver us to the 2030s when, depending on what happens in the 2020s, we will see the emergence of another age.

Whether that new age is our next evolutionary step, or a collapse of civilization, really depends on how much humanity can make unprecedented, yet essential, changes during the 2020s. The historic significance of this decade is that consequential. It is the final decade of this huge historical transit.

In the last 15 years, I became known as the futurist who declared that humanity has exited the Information Age and entered the Shift Age. I have written several books, and innumerable columns and blog posts, about it.

https://davidhoule.com/evolutionshift-blog

Amazon David Houle Author page:
https://www.amazon.com/David-Houle/e/B004I0VO3A/ref=dp_byline_cont_book_1

The Shift Age

We now live in the Shift Age, a time of transformation that will be regarded by future historians as one of the most significant periods in human history. The Shift Age is one of those inflection points or times when much of humanity will change how we live, how we think, how we interact with each other, and what we do. It will even be a time of an emerging new consciousness for many of us.

Shift is everywhere. Think about all of the shifts you're seeing happen today. How we communicate with each other. The way the new global economy is reshaping national and even local markets. What we do for a living. The values we hold. The way we raise and educate our young. The way we view the world. The way we access information and knowledge. The way we influence and are influenced by social concepts.

In the Shift Age, the speed of change has accelerated to the point where change has become environmental. Change is no longer one of several dynamics that we must manage, it is the environment in which we live. We feel it. We are constantly confronted with change. The planned obsolescence of the Industrial Age has given way to the ever more rapid speed of technological and innovation obsolescence. We now suffer from what I call innovation fatigue.

The current iteration of humanity is known as Modern Humanity. It is generally accepted that the age of Modern Humanity began some 150,000 years ago. For most of this time, humanity scarcely differed from other animals – simply trying to survive day to day by hunting and gathering.

Then, approximately 10,000 years ago, some groups of humans started to put down roots and the Agricultural Age began. This led to the placed-based development of society and culture. This 10,000-year period represents most of recorded human history. It is when all the great civilizations came into being. The basic foundation of human society was developed during the Agricultural Age.

The Agricultural Age continued until the 1700s when the invention of the steam engine ushered in the Industrial Age. This age brought about mechanization, urbanization, centralization and a dramatic increase in global wealth. The Industrial Age spanned roughly 250 years until, in the last quarter of the 20th century, the Information Age began in developed countries.

Now let's think about the experience of change in these ages. Accept for the sake of easy math, that a lifetime is 50 years. (We obviously live longer than that now, but centuries and certainly millennia ago we did not.) If a lifetime is 50 years, then 150,000 years, the time Modern Humans has been on this planet, is 3,000 lifetimes. The Agricultural Age, 10,000 years in length, represents 200 lifetimes. So for the first 2,800 of Modern Humanity's lifetimes, we were essentially nomadic and lived in portable housing or in caves. For 200 lifetimes we tilled the land and created civilization, and for only five lifetimes we have lived in the Industrial Age. Finally, it is during the lifetimes of most adults alive today that humanity has lived in the Information Age.

Modern Humans therefore have spent 2,800 lifetimes living in caves, 200 lifetimes tilling the land and creating all the great civilizations of the world, five lifetimes creating all the wonders of the Industrial Age and only a single lifetime living in the Information Age. When we look at our species in the context of this timeline, our current concepts of what constitutes "humanity" and "society" are recent. Many of our reference points come from the last 2,000 years (if one includes the old religions of the world). And even more from just the last 50 years.

Our "Ages" are changing ever more rapidly. During the first 2,800 lifetimes, humanity had no sense of the speed of change. Survival was the only issue. Even during the Agricultural Age, the speed of change was hardly noticeable in a single lifetime. People lived in the same place and held the same occupation as their parents. The average life expectancy was 45 years. In the last few centuries of the Agricultural Age, exploration and discovery started to accelerate social, cultural and economic evolution around the world. The Renaissance in Europe, the great Mayan and Aztec civilizations of Central America, and the sophisticated dynasties in China and India all occurred toward the last quarter of the Agricultural Age. Even during these great strides forward, humans experienced little change in a lifetime.

It was not until the beginning of the Industrial Age that the speed of change was experienced by humanity on a large scale. In the United States, for example, if you were born in the year 1825, you grew up in an essentially agricultural society. The majority of the population lived in the country or in small towns, and land and products from it determined wealth.

By your 60th birthday, if you lived that long, manufacturing began to supplant farming, cities were undergoing explosive growth, you could travel by train and you could have your photograph taken. The world you lived in was noticeably different than that of your grandparents. My grandparents grew up in a world of steam engines, candlelight and horse and buggy. I grew up in a world of television, jet planes, and communication satellites. My son grew up with video games, computers, cell phones, digital media and the Internet.

Therefore, it is only in the last five or six lifetimes that the speed of change could be clearly perceived within a single lifetime. This is essential to remember, as the awareness and experience of the speed of change as a phenomenon is common to practically every human alive today.

So new ages begin and develop for a time before the majority of the population perceives that it is living in a new age. I submit that the Shift Age began around 2006 or mid-decade. It has been interesting to me that when I first started to speak about this new age in 2007, people had a hard time perceiving that they were in a new age. By 2011, after a four-year reorganizational recession, audiences have largely accepted that a new age is upon us as everything had changed or shifted so much in such a short period of time. Welcome to the Shift Age.

This does not mean that when people realize a new age has begun that they easily accept it. When a new age is born, it seems radical, transformative and is often resisted as unnatural, immoral or threatening. This is due to our patterns and habits of thought. We know what we know, we live in a time when things are the way they are. To think differently is difficult. Eventually, reality as we have known it is shown to no longer be true. We find out that facts that we've accepted are not really facts, just beliefs.

10,000 years ago, the concept of humans staying in one place, growing food and creating the tools to do so, was a radical idea that slowly emerged. Staying in one place, and not following the animals and the weather, must have seemed unnatural. The Agricultural Age took many millennia to become the dominant

11

way of life. Once it was, then towns and cities superseded migrant tribes. These led to the development of the Concept of Place. People spent entire lives living in a single place for the first time in humankind's period on Earth.

Once lives started to revolve around place, then civilization arose. Social rules, culture and mores were established to organize these place-based, agriculturally driven civ-ilizations. Place became defining. People were from a place. This led to the orientation of land as the dominant form of wealth. Wealth came from the land.

The Industrial Age triggered massive change. People left the land for the rapidly growing cities. Machines became dominant. Factories created a centralized work force. The concepts of jobs and management began. The factory was the model and production superseded the land as a form and measurement of wealth creation. Those that controlled production created unprecedented wealth. Robber Barons in every country created vast wealth and hundreds of thousands of jobs. Land was no longer solely the place on which crops were grown, but the place from which minerals and fossil fuels were extracted. Cities grew explosively as the poor who worked the land before could now earn more money in cities and factories.

The Industrial Age gave us all the machines and inventions we now take for granted: automobiles, electricity, elevators, airplanes, and untold numbers of production related machinery. This economic reorganization initiated new social structures including public school systems, transportation systems, organized sports, private clubs, civic and charitable organizations, and everything related to the automobile. The Industrial Age organized the developed countries of the world into an order that, in large part, defined the 19th and 20th centuries (and is still largely in place today).

The Industrial Age migrated the Concept of Place from small towns to the City. At the same time, communications technologies were invented, and they made the world "smaller". The Telegraph was replaced by the Telephone. Radio was followed by Television. The world became more connected. World War II was the first radio war. Viet Nam was the first television war.

Then, in the 1970s computers were transformed. While mainframe computers continued to exist – though often updated for processing speed – we started to use mini-computers, then desktop computers, then laptops and finally hand-held devices. All are in use today. Satellites expanded global communications and created new business models including cable television. The fax machine, the electronic calculator and the copier changed office work. That was when we realized that the Information Age was upon us.

Since the Information Age began approximately 50 to 60 years ago in developed countries, the perception of the speed of change has become pronounced. The future is showing up at an accelerating rate. Alvin Toffler's book "Future Shock" was published in 1970. The simple premise of the book was that humanity was entering a period when time is accelerating – new inventions will arrive and "shock" us into the future. One personal example was in the mid-1980s when I saw a man walking down the street talking on one of those early five pound cell phones. Wow, a phone without a cord being used on the street! That is the future!

In the decades since 1970, humanity has come to accept this future shock as an almost constant experience. We settle into learning and adapting to a new technology and its enabling power in our lives, and then almost immediately a new technological breakthrough or gadget renders what we just mastered dated or even obsolete. We say we embrace innovation, and yet at times it overwhelms us. We want to keep up, and in most areas of our lives we do, but there always seems to be a part of our lives where we can't quite catch up. Things come at us too fast and with great force… we are drinking from the proverbial fire hose. This sense of the rapidity of change really began in the past 25 years, a transitional time when humanity moved from what was to what will be.

Change can be quite unsettling. What we "know" and the technologies we use are our current reality. We all tend to develop a sense of comfort in what is, what is known, how we live, what the current parameters and ways of living are. So when some change or sense of disruption is felt, we often get anxious. In reality the only constant in the universe is change. In our most recent history, the speed of change and the depth of our sense of disruption has been increasing.

The Three Forces of The Shift Age

In 2007 when "The Shift Age" was published, I first suggested that the three major flows of the age were:

1. The Flow to Global

2. The Flow to the Individual

3. The Accelerating Electronic Connectedness of Humanity

Much of the change we have been living through can be linked back to one or more of these flows.

The Flow to Global

The Flow to Global goes far beyond the global economy. We have replaced the words 'foreign', 'overseas', and 'international' with the word 'global'. We think in terms of global constructs. More importantly, we have entered the global stage of human evolution. Our sense of social groupings has grown ever larger. We have moved from family to tribe to village to city to city state and then to nation state. Our only boundary now is planetary. The biggest problems, issues and dynamics we face are all global in nature. This flow is irreversible. Sure, there are retreats into nationalism, but they are only the last death knell of the nation state. The 21st century will be known as the time humanity left the era of the nation state, which has largely been time congruent to the Industrial Age.

The Flow to the Individual

We are each more powerful as individuals than ever before. This is due to several things, most important of which is the explosion of choice. 50 years ago, in the United States and other developed countries there were maybe 15 brands of cereals, and two to four television networks, so choice was limited and time constrained. Today there are dozens and dozens of cereal brands, 500+ channels on television, unlimited web sites and all available 24 hours a day.

In addition, there has been an explosion of free agency in the workplace. Ever-growing electronic connectivity and increasing bandwidth have helped to migrate power from institutions to individuals. Gatekeepers are disappearing, disintermediation and its primary agent, the Internet, have reorganized the economic landscape. The individual has become the primary economic unit, the micro-micro that is combining with the macro-macro of the flow to global. We are distinct individuals who are global citizens.

Accelerating Electronic Connectedness

This has, is and will be through much of the 2020s, the single most powerful flow for humanity. This means the Internet, but even more so, handheld devices. As of the end of 2019 there are 7.7 billion people alive and roughly 70% of them have some sort of handheld device. As of the beginning of the 2020s, more people have these devices than indoor plumbing. Another way to state this is that there are several hundred million people who both live in poverty and have handheld devices.

This must be viewed within a historical context. It is about 170 years ago that the telegraph was widely deployed. This means that for the 150,000 years that Modern Humanity has lived on earth, only $1/10,000^{th}$ of one percent of this time have we been able to communicate in real time without being face to face. Another way to think of this is that more people listen to a recording of Mozart in a day in 2020 than ever listened to Mozart during his entire lifetime – as one had to be in the same room as Mozart back then to hear him.

These three flows are the underpinnings of much of the change we have and are experiencing:

- The reality that there is no longer any time, distance, or place limiting human communication.

- The 24-hour reality of the global economy.

- The on-demand economy of whatever we want, whenever and wherever we want it.

- The move from a place-based mentality and consciousness to a space-based mentality and consciousness. Think of the Cloud, which is accessible when and where we need it.

This brings us to 2010 – 2020, the first full decade of The Shift Age.

Chapter Two 2010-2019:

The First Decade of 21st Century Thought

On Friday January 1, 2010 I posted a column on my blog entitled "The Transformation Decade". It blew up in the blogosphere and on Twitter, so I had a couple of days of feeling self-congratulatory that my moniker for this new decade was so widely embraced.

Here is the dictionary definition of transformation: "change in form, appearance, nature or character."

So, 2010 -2020 would be the decade where much of human life would be changing form, appearance, nature or character. As a futurist speaking to hundreds of CEOs every year, and also leading corporate retreats about the future, I found myself saying to CEOs that: "*you must change the form, appearance, nature or character of your business if you want to have a business in 2020*". This has largely been borne out. Since 2010, many business sectors have undergone significant changes; especially media, communications, retail and housing.

Why is 2010 - 2020 the first decade of 21st Century Thought?

Yes, 2000 (2001 if you are being a stickler) was the first year of the third millennium. However, society, culture, tech-nology, business, and most significantly, legacy thinking does not ever fully and neatly align with the calendar.

"Legacy thinking" is a term I coined in 2012 in "Entering the Shift Age". I posited that we had entered a time when legacy thinking was collapsing. Legacy thinking is viewing the present and future through thoughts from the past. A simple metaphor for this would be the act of rowing a boat. You are looking back to where you have been with your back facing where you are going. You are backing into the future, looking at the past.

The last decade began the wholesale collapse of legacy thinking. It will be completed in ways large and small in the 2020s

Remember the '60s?

The '60s we remember did not start in January 1960. It began with the assassination of President Kennedy on November 22, 1963, followed three months later by the Beatles performing on the Ed Sullivan show, and then the escalation of the Viet Nam war. So "the 60s" began a third of the way through the decade. Prior to these three significant events, the early 1960s looked and sounded a lot like the 1950s.

There's a similar paradigm with our new century and millennium. Humanity powered into the new century with the conceptual constructs of the prior one. It was not until the second decade that we really started having 21st century thoughts. Thoughts that would not have occurred to us in the 20th century.

The 20th Century

If you think of the 20th century as "the century of science", the "century of World Wars', or "the American Century", it all began in the years 1914 -18. That's when WW I (the first industrialized war), the Russian Revolution, the General Theory of Relativity, and the current maps of Europe and the Middle East were born. So many of the story lines of the last century began in its second decade.

Future historians will look back on 2010-2019 as the first decade of 21st century thought. It was the decade when the transformations and disruptions of this new age and century have brought us to now the 2020s.

To refresh your memory, here are some things that happened in the last decade that upset legacy thinking in various ways:

- The "cloud" as a shared storage space.

- A majority of the world's population connected to the Internet.

- Billions of people with hand-held devices more powerful than supercomputers of the 1980s.
- The concept that one can buy anything on-line and have it quickly delivered to one's home.

- The introduction of Augmented and Virtual Realities.

- #Metoo

- Streaming video on demand.

The 2020s, the last decade of the Shift Age, will usher in the greatest quantity of change, creative destruction, and disruption of any decade in human history. It will be as disruptive as any 20 to 30 year period in history.

The Collapse of Legacy Thinking

During the Transformation Decade, legacy thinking largely collapsed. In this first decade of 21st century thought, the conceptual constructs of the 20th century began to collapse. Old physical realities collapsed in the face of new digital ones.

Think of the major disruptions of this decade: communications, media, computing, retail, housing, new work definitions, new gender definitions, the dis-intermediation of "go-between" entities, the reduction of costs and the globalization of practically everything.

This is why it was the Transformation Decade: the conceptual constructs and the physical realities put in place over the 20th century were "changing their nature, shape, character and form". In fact, this is the first century when humanity, particularly the developed world, has to go back and retrofit the legacy infrastructure of the last century. Hierarchies evolved into networks, centralization morphed into decentralization, consciousness moved from place to space, distribution channels migrated onto the Internet. Computing became mobile and ubiquitous.

In the 20th century, humanity quadrupled its population, paved much of the planet, built suburbia, globalized the internal combustion engine and fossil fuel use, and created content distribution platforms including radio, microwave, television and early satellite communications. It had taken 150,000 years to reach a global population of one billion people around 1800, which grew to one and a half billion by 1900. There were massive amounts of uncharted, undeveloped land on all continents. "Go west young man!" (usually attributed to New York Tribune editor Horace Greeley), was a catch phrase for Manifest Destiny in the America of the 1800s. Now 30% of the U.S. population lives west of the Rockies.

Now in the Shift Age, and the early third of the 21st Century, we are having to repurpose so much of the installed base of the last century. Warehouses are being converted to loft living spaces, riverfronts are transformed from industrial sites to parks and entertainment venues, and physical retail spaces are mostly sitting empty waiting for a resurrection (I suggest vertical indoor vegetable farms).

This was the decade when, for the first time in history, humanity had to learn to manage two realities: the physical reality and the screen reality. This is a critical concept to understand as it underlies much about generations, communications, destruction of physical markets, attention and consciousness.

The Shift Age was the first time that humanity had to adapt to a dual reality. In ages prior there was only the physical reality. Starting with the ubiquity of laptops and then mobile phones, we all gained a second life: a screen reality.

This duality is often called the physical/digital realities. I like to use the term screen reality because it is where we experience our digital reality: on screens.

Our screen realities are disrupting our physical realities. Why have there been dozens of bankruptcies of iconic retailers, thousands of store closings and hundreds of malls closing over the last 10 years? Due to the screen reality of Amazon.com. Airbnb, Uber and other interactive platforms are disrupting our physical reality. This is something that traditional businesses, founded in physical placeness, have learned the hard way. Too many businesses have continued to view their competitors as other physical businesses... not understanding that their ultimate competition is in the screen reality.

Increasingly, the new, the transformative, the disruptive changes we are experiencing are products of our screen realities.

This also infuses the intense and significant differences between the generations.

Digital Natives, born since 1998 in the US and somewhat later in other countries, ARE the first generation to spend all of their lives within these physical/screen dual realities. Prior generations grew up in physical, place-based reality. We all have stories about young children who are completely, intuitively adept at navigating the screen reality. I have spoken to numerous grandparents for whom tech support is their grandkids.

Think of the differences in consciousness between Digital Natives and their parents, between them as students and their adult teachers. This is a much discussed technological generation gap. This gap causes hand wringing in older generations about the "screen addiction" of the young. "They don't read. They are becoming anti-social. They are depressed." We have all heard these statements, but they expressed through the lens of older generations who are digital and screen immigrants.

Boomers and GenXers control the media and academia, 10-year-olds don't, so the discussion on all these issues must be viewed through this generational filter. As I will suggest in the last two chapters of this book, discerning the sea changes between the boomer generation and the three generations that follow provides a peek into the arc of our collective future.

It is axiomatic that any new technology disrupts existing reality. The automobile transformed landscapes over much of the planet. Television changed social and family behaviors and created McLuhan's Global Village. The computer changed every aspect of the workplace and then the home. Then came the Internet, the greatest force of disintermediation since Gutenberg invented the moveable type press.

If, in 1970, I had told you that in the future we would all have hand-held devices that fit into a jeans pocket, each of which has more computing power than NASA had back then, would you have believed me? Then, if I assured you that it was going to happen, and asked you if human behavior would change as a result, I think your answer would be, "Yes!"

Now we have that reality. So why should we be surprised that the hand-held device is changing behavior everywhere?

The 2010-2020 decade of transformation has delivered us to the 2020s.

Chapter 3 – The Futurist Becomes the Canary in the Mine

In 2015 - 2016 I stood down from traveling around the world speaking about the future to publish a book on climate change and then to set up a global non-profit to create "crew consciousness" for Spaceship Earth.[1] After two years of deep research and education on climate change, it became clear to me that it would be a dereliction of my duty as a professional futurist if I did not speak about climate change. It is simply impossible to address the future of humanity without speaking urgently about climate change. More on this later in the book.

---

[1] https://thisspaceshipearth.org/

In 2017, I went back into the world delivering presentations about humanity's general future… my primary occupation. I realized that I had forgotten about a firm statement I had made 10 years earlier: in the Shift Age, the speed of change would accelerate to the point where it was no longer a linear line, but that change would become environmental. All aspects of our lives would be in simultaneous states of change. In 2010, I announced that the speed of technological change was the slowest it would be for the rest of our lifetimes.

As I prognosticated about the 2017 to 2030 timeframe, I realized that humanity's future in this new century would be determined during this 13-year period. It became apparent to me that massive change and disruption were about to occur, and it became all I could focus on. I could not get out of my head the famous and apocalyptic statement of R. Buckminster Fuller from 1970:

"In several decades, humanity will come to a fork in the road, and will have to choose between utopia or oblivion."

Not only had humanity reached the fork in the road, but we had mindlessly started down the path to oblivion. I remember a speech I gave at a technology college, when, speaking about imminent and massive change, I said that I felt like both a futurist and the proverbial canary in the mine.

It is that clear and deep sense of imminent, historically unprecedented disruption that has led to this series of books about the 2020s. We have entered a decade that will, depending on how we navigate it, largely shape the 21st century.

The highest value I can bring to the world – to businesses, governments, associations and individuals – is to be right about the future. If I cannot provide a correct sense of direction, accurate forecasts, and provoke people to think about the future in new ways, then I am not of value.

Futurists are often called to look decades into the future. I have done that and continue to do so. However, given that the speed of change has now become environmental, it is clear to me that to look beyond the 2020s is a fool's errand. What is about to happen, the massively important choices we will have to collectively face, the huge unknowns of such things as climate change and technological intelligence, mean that the future has been accelerating to NOW. The future is now. Now is the time to leave the mine.

We are at that inflection point, the nexus of change, the historical moment which will set civilization on its path for the remainder of the 21st century. The 2020s will define the direction for humanity, including our survival as a species.

One of the real problems facing humanity today is the belief that what we perceive as reality will continue. To state this relative to the Fuller quote, we have already started down the path to oblivion. We are not aware of where we are headed, or even fully aware of where we are. We pay little heed to the massive changes going on around us. We tend to think of these big, new events as exceptions to the reality we cling to, not an emerging new reality. We are therefore always behind, in reaction mode, not anticipating or taking proactive actions. This is why, as a futurist, I feel urgency to sound the alarm!

Alarm, not because that is the sentiment needed, but more a loud, ringing warning that we must, in this moment in history, fully accept that this is the most critical moment in recorded history... and that the canary has died.

We must quickly exit the mine. The mine of legacy thinking, 20th century conceptual constructs, and the mine of emotional attachment to the memories of the past. Our belief systems and our perceptions of reality are no longer valid.

"We look at the present through a rear-view mirror. We march backwards into the future." – Marshall McLuhan

To stay with that metaphor, my job as a futurist is to see and then share the view through the windshield, looking ahead up the road.

The future can only be seen and understood by being fully in the present. I embrace the Buddhist practice of being fully in the moment. That is where the future is occurring. A perfect quote on this:

"The future is here, it is just not evenly distributed." – William Gibson

As a futurist I attract, and am attracted to, people from around the world who are thinking and writing about various aspects of our collective future. Many of these people are brilliant and driven by a love for something at risk of being destroyed due to ignorance. Over the past few years, the number of these people has been rapidly growing. A critical mass is developing in many fields of human endeavor: climate change activists, technological intelligence engineers, genetic researchers, spiritual elders, conscious capitalists, space explorers and all forms of hackers (bio / life / environmental / intelligence / cyber). As a futurist, I see it as my challenge to synthesize all these areas into the over-arching trends and contexts that can provide cohesive thinking about the truly big challenges and opportunities we face, now, here in the 2020s.

We now must exit the mine of legacy thinking, of holding on, of resisting disruptive change in order to see where we truly are.

Chapter 4 - Entering the Global Stage of Human Evolution

We are now in the global stage of human evolution.

The Flow to Global was mentioned in Chapter 1. It is one of three flows of the Shift Age. The label "global" has become common. In the last century the words used were "overseas" "foreign" "international". The concept of global is now something we all live with.

The Flow to Global reflects the fact that we have entered the global stage of human evolution. There is no going back. We have moved organizationally from family to tribe to village to city to city state to the nation state and now our only boundaries are global. This is true across most aspects of humanity: issues, climate, economics, culture and consciousness.

First a historical step back...

The era of the nation state has largely been time congruent with the Industrial Age. There were nations in the Agricultural Age, but it was only in the last 250 years that humanity moved toward the nation state as the highest organizational form of government. Most problems were within nations or due to the aggression between them. Nationalism ruled. Economics, money, education, health care, culture, language all were nation state defined. People felt themselves citizens of their country first and foremost.

Post WWII, the United Nations was created to provide a global political platform with the hope that it would promote peace and support higher human goals. It was an organization of nation members, but it had no true authority over nations. The evidence of that is clear: the Korean War, the Vietnam War, the first Iraq war, Bosnia, and the still on-going, at the time of this writing, conflicts in Iraq/Afghanistan/Iran/Pakistan. The Security Council, made up of a small group of nations, had authority and power, but the reality was that the Cold War meant there was always contention based upon the divide between the "communist" and "free" states.

This nation state reality is still in existence. The problem now, though, is that the biggest problems humanity faces are truly global in nature. (*NOTE TO READER: the final draft of this book is being written while "staying in place" because of COVID-19. The virus does not respect national boundaries.*) Climate change, immigration, wealth inequality, pollution, ocean degradation and social injustice are all issues that are larger than any single nation. They are global problems that need global solutions.

Nations are not structured to face global problems, so there have been efforts to collaborate to face them. This is not working very well. The wars listed above are a case in point. A more recent example is the vestiges of the Conference of the Parties (COP) Climate forums. Designed to foster the cooperation between nations needed to effectively address our climate crisis, the COP has devolved into bureaucratic meetups sponsored in part by the fossil fuel industry. A chapter later in this book focuses on our climate crisis. Hopefully, the Paris Climate Accord is the last time we approach a global problem as a collection of nation states.

The Paris Climate Accord of 2015 was a massive effort, thought successful at the time, for 195 countries to come together and commit to facing carbon reduction. Kumbaya! We did it! Hurray for us! That was the feeling at the time. The flaw was, to get consensus, the goals had to be lowered and dumbed down so all could sign. Consensus typically results in suboptimal solutions. The commitments were less than the science at the time recommended.

Since that temporary celebration five years ago, not one of the larger countries has met their promised carbon reduction goals. Talk, no action. In addition, the goal of the Accord was to keep a global temperature rise this century well below 2 degrees Celsius above pre-industrial levels, and to pursue efforts to limit the temperature increase even further to 1.5 degrees Celsius. Due to almost total non-compliance by the signatories, it is expected that 1.5 Celsius will be reached by 2022 or 2023. It is already 1.3 degrees Celsius in some parts of the planet. It was at 1 degree Celsius in 2015 when the Accord was signed.

Tragically, this COP accord fell even further behind with a total failure to reach consensus in the late-2019 meeting in Barcelona. So, it is a painful indication of our need to move to a more global level of issue by issue governance. This will be examined in a subsequent book in this series. A quick comment on this need and how it will manifest itself. This 30 to 40 year move from nation state centric government to global centric government will begin with issues. The nations will, one global issue/problem at a time, move toward coordinated, collaborative addressing of the issue. It will probably start with Climate Change, then Natural Resources, then migration and of course global integrated public health. A daily, virtual, screen reality gathering of the leading authorities, signed off on by the nation states, that meets every day in an "assembly" or "committee" in the screen reality to coordinate and set global policy on the specific issue.

The Global Stage of Human Evolution

The 21st Century is a huge and deeply significant transition to this new global stage of human evolution. In fact, this new stage underpins the remaining chapters of this book.

Every aspect of human life is being integrated into an ever more connected global reality. The entire 150,000 year history of Modern Humanity has brought us to this next stage of Homo Sapiens' evolutionary journey.

It took our entire history to reach one billion in 1800. By 1900, human population had increased by 50% to 1.5 billion. Then it doubled in the next 50 years to three billion by 1950. Now, 70 years later we stand – at the time of the writing of this book in early 2020 – at 7.77 billion. This is an increase of 260% in the lifetime of this author. So, for roughly 149,800 years the growth was one billion. In 200 years, we increased that by 776%. We have only one planet and now we are everywhere on it, so we have simply populated ourselves into this new stage of human evolution.

While our population has been exploding, man has migrated all over the planet. Add to this an ever increasing electronic connectedness between people, and the result is a degree of global integration without precedent.

Immigration has become a problem experienced all over the world. In the past half-decade, there has been an increasing reaction to this global flow, with rising nationalism and populism. This is a political reaction, led by politicians who are using fear of a new reality to mobilize people to want to "go back" to "the better days of the past"... a time when people understood their world. Resistance to the new is something politicians frequently use to maintain the status quo. The status quo is only a temporary solace and is, in fact, an illusion.

The only constant in the universe is change. That is why the status quo never holds. The current status quo of the largely 20th century view of nation states is therefore soon to give way to the new dynamics and structures of a more globally integrated human existence at every level.

We are now all, to a greater or lesser degree, global citizens. We travel everywhere. In 1950 the total number of global travelers, defined as those traveling internationally (not for business) was one million. In 2015 that number was one billion, a thousand-fold increase. Many people now travel thousands of miles in a day.

We are ever more connected individually via technology. Again, it was only in the last 200 years, with the invention and global deployment of the telegraph that Modern Humanity could communicate without being face to face. We often forget what this means from a historical perspective. 200 years ago, it could take weeks for a letter to get from sender to recipient, and weeks for a return response. The telegraph brought that down to hours.

Today there are close to six billion cell phones in use, which translates into 86% of all people over the age of 15. To a significant degree, communications back and forth anywhere in the world takes just seconds. There is no time, distance or place limit to communication anymore.

Many of us alive today have trouble embracing the future. It has been forgotten how far we have traveled in the last two centuries. Our current reality is not old, but new. In almost every aspect of human life, the reality we live in now did not exist in the 1980s.

Billons of people connected via speed of light fiber optics and satellites, is a reality that just came to be over the past decade. Never before have we all been so connected by communications and information immediacy. This connectedness is the foundation for the global age of human evolution.

History is accelerating. During most of human history, civilizations were unaware of each other. Let's arbitrarily pick the first several centuries after Christ. The Roman Civilization in Europe, the Mayan Civilization in Central and South America and the Han, Wei and Jin Dynasties in Asia all existed at the same time. Yet they were completely unaware of each other.

Prior to the end of the 19th century, civilizations worldwide may have been aware of each other through trade or war, but were not connected by any information flow. Humanity is now moving to a space-based consciousness because we are all connected and what happens 15,000 miles away is knowable in seconds. This results in an acceleration of interaction, response, creativity and awareness that is new.

The deep psychological underpinning of this move to the global stage of human evolution was the earthrise photo taken by astronaut William Anders from Apollo 8 on December 24, 1968.

As Apollo 14 astronaut Edgar Mitchell claimed:

"You develop an instant global consciousness, a people orientation, an intense dissatisfaction with the state of the world and a compulsion to do something about it. From out there on the moon, international politics looks so petty."

So, our current ease of travel, accelerating connectedness, realization of Spaceship Earth as a common living space, plus the number and significance of global issues we are facing, all place us in a new global stage of evolution. And we will never go back.

If you feel some resistance to this idea, please go back and read the four quotes at the front of the book.

Chapter 5 - The Beginning of the Age of Intelligence

The 2020s will be the decade when the entire concept, definition, understanding and use of intelligence will change. By the end of the decade we will have entered a completely new landscape of intelligence, one that will illustrate our next evolutionary step [Chapter 9].

Throughout history, humankind has thought of itself as the most intelligent of all species. Because we are mammals, we have attributed intelligence of varying degrees to other mammals. Our definition of intelligence is limited… one that is completely anthropocentric. It is this narrow view that has and will limit our ability to see a truer, fuller, more technological and even cosmic intelligence that we are discovering and creating.

We are 70 years into the age of computing, 25 years into the age of the Internet, and a decade into the real age of what is called Artificial Intelligence. We are only a few years into the greatest neurological breakthroughs in history. For the past 50 years neuroscientists have been claiming that "we have learned more about the brain in the last 10 years than all the time before". This quote will continue to be true through most of the 2020s. Neuroscience is that new and quickly developing. It's the last frontier of medical knowledge. By the end of this decade though, we may have fully mapped the brain, and then the next frontier will be consciousness [Chapter 10].

To simplify intelligence into three loose categories:

1. Exploration and information gathering about the human brain and how to use this new knowledge.

2. Development of Technological Intelligence.

3. The symbiotic merger of #1 and #2.

Neuroscience

The 2020s will bring a nearly complete understanding of the human brain and how it works. By the end of this decade, we will have fully mapped the brain. We will be using this new knowledge to better treat all kinds of neurological diseases and conditions. The scientific field of brain health will be firmly established. For years we used phrases like "heart-healthy" relative to diet, exercise and lifestyle. We are now beginning to use a "brain-healthy" label for these same categories.

Mental health will be transformed. The mind/body duality will finally be integrated in terms of how conditions including schizophrenia, depression, anxiety, bipolar disorder, obsessive-compulsive disorder, and a host of others will be treated.

The NIH suggests that fully 20% of the U.S. population suffers from a mental disorder at any point in time. "Four of the 10 leading causes of disability – major depression, bipolar

disorder, schizophrenia, and obsessive-compulsive disorder —
are mental illnesses."[1]

This complete mapping of the brain will have significant public
health and productivity benefits. It will also play an ever-larger
part in the field of longevity.

As we come to more fully understand the entire brain, its
neural interconnectedness and processing speed, we will make
exponential progress in computing. For years data processing
engineers have heralded the dawn of quantum computing and
neural networks. This should lead to explosively faster and
more powerful computers.

In the mid-20th century, the pioneers of computing created a
binary structure that exists to this day. Computers have
become immensely quicker and more robust. Yet our brains
still function at a faster rate than super computers. Computers
will catch up. When they do, will they resemble our brains in
functionality? Will these new computing devices and pathways
launch entirely new forms of computing? The general answer
is yes. Ray Kurzweil's "Singularity" will occur, the only
question is timing and scale.[2]

The larger question is how those at the cutting edge of brain
science can effectively interact with those at the cutting edge
of Technological Intelligence to map, replicate and then
surpass the processes and speed of the human brain. This
merging of expertise will reveal entirely new realms of
Intelligence and the application of that intelligence.

[1] https://www.medicinenet.com/script/main/art.asp

[2] https://www.kurzweilai.net/futurism-ray-kurzweil-claims-
singularity-will-happen-by-2045

The Age of Intelligence will result in:

- A complete mapping and full understanding of how the brain works.

- The use of this knowledge to enhance brain functionality and brain health.

- Leveraging of this knowledge to create new forms of medical treatments that are brain centric.

- Implantation of chips for memory and the treatment of chronic diseases.

- External inputs for treatment of chronic conditions.

- Interaction with Technological Intelligence to create new levels of computational power and speed.

Technological Intelligence

In choosing the name Technological Intelligence as opposed to Artificial Intelligence, I know I am swimming upstream against the current of colloquial use of the latter term. Let me explain.

In 2015 and early 2016, I was having a problem with the conversation about Artificial Intelligence. AI had a basic duality of reputation – a freeing of human capital alongside incredible abundance, versus a dystopic view of robotic overlords and Terminator-like futures.

I looked up the word "intelligence" in several dictionaries. None of them had the word 'human' in the definitions. Here is the definition of intelligence from Dictionary.com:

- *capacity for learning, reasoning, understanding, and similar forms of mental activity;*

- *aptitude in grasping truths, relationships, facts, meanings;*

- *manifestation of a high mental capacity: "He writes with intelligence and wit";*

- *the faculty of understanding;*

- *knowledge of an event, circumstance, etc., received or imparted;*

- *news, information;*

- *the gathering or distribution of information, especially secret information.*

The word "human" does not appear in the dictionary definition of intelligence. Dolphins are intelligent. Whales are intelligent. Elephants are intelligence. Intelligence exists outside humanity.

So why do we call it "artificial intelligence"? Calling something artificial implies that it is not as good as real. The only time in my life when I embraced artificial is when, at a ski resort in the 1990s, there was no real snow, so the resort created artificial snow on several runs. In every other instance in my life, artificial implied something less than real.

The phrase Artificial Intelligence implies that it is less than real. Less than human or not as good as. Over the last five years I used the term Technological Intelligence (TI), not Artificial Intelligence (AI).

Another legacy phrase is "Machine Learning". This refers to the evolutionary point when technological intelligence no longer needs to be taught. It teaches itself. Why "machine"? Who thinks of their computers as machines?

We think of our computers as hardware, which is fueled by software. We refer to 'the cloud'. We have become so technologically oriented that we use tech terms to describe humans. We download, we upload, we interface with, we reprogram, we reboot, we occupy virtual worlds. We use language and the imagery of technology when describing human behavior. Yet, when it comes to intelligence, we diminish what is not human.

Even the most ardently excited scientists in the field of technological intelligence, perhaps unwittingly, use language that diminishes the field they are exploring. Thinking in dualities always leaves something out or misses something. Phrases like right or wrong, good or evil, yin or yang are humanity's effort to place structure on an infinite universe, the better to comprehend it. Human intelligence and artificial intelligence as a duality has this anthro-pomorphic blind spot.

The contention here is that by using the word artificial in front of the word intelligence we are on a sub-conscious, sub-lingual level denigrating the entire science. This is one of the reasons there is concern about it. It is not US!

Another form of "otherism" to create separation. Often it is "us" versus "them". Here, with the use of the word "artificial" it is "us" versus "it".

Technological Intelligence in the 2020s

Technological intelligence has long been a vision of science fiction writers and the more visionary scientists in the field. During these past 60 years it has moved forward in fits and starts, but until this past decade has never begun to match these visions. Now it is.

In the past 25 years, there have been some general, historical breakthroughs, at least in how technological intelligence compares to human intelligence.

In 1997 the reigning world chess champion, Garry Kasparov played against IBM's Big Blue computer and lost the full match. This was huge news. In prior competitions, the computer had won a game, or two, but never a full match. It was the first time that a computer had ever beaten a grand master... Kasparov is still considered the greatest chess grand master of all time.

A human grandmaster has not beaten Big Blue (now Watson) since 1997. In fact, today the best chess programs consistently beat grandmasters even when working atop off the shelf computer hardware.

Of course, a primary reason for this technological dominance is that computers are capable of playing hundreds of thousands of games in a short amount of time to constantly learn from past mistakes. Computers have a computational advantage

In 2011, Watson easily beat the two top Jeopardy players. This is a different paradigm... not merely computational. This was a mastery of contextual, cultural, historical and social knowledge. Even the Jeopardy requirement to framing the answer as a question displayed a new level of cognition.

In early 2016, Google's AlphaGo, played a five game match against Lee Sedol, the 18 time Go world champion from South Korea. Go is a completely different playing field from chess. As Google stated at the time, the number of possible moves on a Go board is the same as the number of atoms in the universe, virtually infinite. Therefore, in addition to computation, there needs to be a sense akin to intuition, to win at Go.

The new piece of computing that AlphaGo incorporated was the use of neural networks which allowed AlphaGo to learn on its own from endless Go games it played against itself... AlphaGo won, 4 to 1.

This, more than anything prior, alerted all to the rapidly growing power of technological intelligence. Google "move 37" to take a deeper dive into the competition. It prompted my conviction that we are entering the Age of Intelligence.

We are in the first year of the 2020s and technological intelligence is growing and improving at an incredible rate. In this decade we will begin to fully experience the visions of those science fiction writers and visionary scientists.

Technological Intelligence and Electricity

In lists of the top inventions of all time, after the wheel and the printing press, electricity is next. Many inventions on the list – including television, computers and the Internet – are reliant on electricity.

Electricity is the one invention that most shaped how humanity lives on the planet (perhaps excepting the wheel). Electricity has enabled us to live anywhere. It runs the air-conditioning units that make it possible to live in places like the Sunbelt in the U.S , the Middle East and Southeast Asia. It gave us electronic media and all sorts of modern-day conveniences like all the electric appliances in our kitchens

Electricity is currently the primary input that most determines how we live on the planet. Technological Intelligence will become its equal in that regard.

Technological intelligence will dramatically change the world of work, self-identity and how humans interact with all things technological. It will enable the greatest unleashing of human potential in history. It will alter all aspects of how humanity lives… in both obvious and unseen ways.

The decade of the 2020s is when TI becomes ever more dominant in, and supportive of, human endeavors. A century from now, historians will look back at the 2020s as the beginning of the Age of Intelligence, and it will be one of the dominant themes of the 21st Century.

Technological Intelligence and Humanity Together

As we enter the 2020s, we are surrounded by TI every day. Examples include automated voice customer service, self-learning algorithms that track our behavior, on-line retail that predicts (often accurately) what we want and need.

We are already living in symbiotic relations with TI. Build on this current reality and we begin to see a personal future where we are always supported, assisted and protected by TI. It will become natural to us to always have these TI extensions and augmentations to ourselves.

"David, do you really want to make this choice? It is different than your past behavior, and it also seems to be the wrong decision based upon current data. Would you like me to explain?"

It is on the larger, transformative issues that TI will dramatically alter our world.

World of Work

There are a wide range of estimates on the percentage of human jobs that will be lost in this decade to TI. Estimates range from 20 to 50% of all jobs in developed countries. Anything repetitive, data driven or based purely on logic is at risk. There has long been a misconception that this disintermediation applies only to what were called "blue-collar" jobs. No longer true. Accountants and lawyers are the two professions often considered at highest risk. The more the work is repetitive, or data based, the higher the probability of

TI taking it over. The more the work requires deep and interactive discernment and emotional intelligence, the lower the probability. For example, therapists are at minimal risk.

Many think that robots are the same as TI. They are not. Robots toil in physical reality. TI often operates in the screen reality. Our fixation on robots is because they are often human-like… having limbs and mobility. Increasingly robots will leverage TI. Again, that anthropocentric view of ours can skew perceptions. We wonder whether robots can emote or feel as do. We are trying to make them in our image and thus over emphasize robots as the "face" of TI.

How "human" will TI become?

Prior to the AlphaGo event in 2016 it was widely believed that TI would never attain any sort of creativity or originality. Since then, with the development of sophisticated self-learning neural networks, it is clear that, TI can "create" in ways that humans think of that term.

The symbolic computer, such as Big Blue that defeated Kasparov in 1997, is developed purely on human input. Symbolic computers are programmed to think logically and make decisions as humans do. This works for massive computational tasks. This type of TI can create art but based upon human input. Music, paintings and graphics can be created, but based upon human input. A symbolic computer can create art, but it will never be fully unique as it is tethered to human input. It is used by artists as a tool.

Neural Networks are based upon the way neurons work in the human brain, and they are able to learn on their own. (This is where Neuroscience breakthroughs will have huge impacts.) It is this subset of TI that will birth original works of art, music and all creative endeavors. Sometime in this decade, the first "Beethoven" or "Mozart" TI will emerge with foundational TI music that will be "music to human ears", but not of humanity.

The most impactful aspect of Technological Intelligence in the 2020s will be the growing symbiosis between humanity and TI. It will grow in power exponentially… and we will need it to navigate the disruptions ahead.

Humanity and TI will forge ahead together *and for mutual benefit*.

The deeper, longer term ramifications of this will be dealt with in Chapter 9.

Chapter 6 – The Critical Decade to Address Climate Change

In many ways, the 2020s will set the course for the 21st century. This will be a reoccurring theme and it is this reality that makes the canary in the mine metaphor apropos. It is absolutely, completely true with the unquestionable, overwhelming existential threat that is climate change.

It is important to understand that the degree of global warming and resultant climate change that is occurring has never happened since homo sapiens have been on Earth. This means that we have no experience, history or concept as to how this will all unfold. More on that a bit later.

In researching and writing of the book I co-authored with Tim Rumage in 2015 "This Spaceship Earth", I was shocked and overwhelmed with the reality of what was happening. So many seemingly irreversible dynamics of collapse were starting to occur. It was the two years working on this book that made it clear to me that it would be a dereliction of my duty and responsibility as a futurist to not speak about climate change.

It is and will be the largest challenge humanity faces in the 2020s.

In 2019 I co-authored a book with Bob Leonard entitled "Moving to a Finite Earth Economy – Crew Manual". There were three motivations for writing this book.

First, it was clear that climate change was happening NOW. It was no longer this cataclysmic event sometime in the future. It was affecting some aspect of humanity every day somewhere on Earth. This meant that finally humanity had to respond, as we had entered the fight or flight stage. Humanity has no innate biological trigger for dealing with some catastrophe that might be a few decades away. It does have genetic wiring for fight or flight in the presence of a clear and present danger. Do we fight the Sabre Tooth tiger or run from it? We believed that now that it was happening, humanity had no choice but to face something unprecedented in human history.

Second, the question about climate change had moved from "is it real?" to "what can we do?" We wrote the book to answer that question. Here is what we have to do, here is how we measure our progress, and here, at all levels of human organization (global, nation state, state and provinces, cities, neighborhoods and individuals) is what we need to do, year by year to make the necessary transition by 2030. Why 2030? Because the feedback loop from the planet keeps indicating that global warming is happening faster than expected.

In the 1990s, climate scientists and those concerned about impending global warming thought that a complete transition away from fossil fuels by 2100 would be sufficient. Because global warming was a novel phenom-enon, the scientists had no precedent to reference. They assumed that warming would be a gradual linear increase.

Then, in the early part of this century, we began to see outcomes that were predicted to happen much later in the century. Severe weather, rising sea levels and melting ice all were happening at a much faster rate than anticipated. So the goal posts were moved in... a complete transition off fossil fuels had to happen by 2050. This is still prevalent thinking today. It is wrong. Changes are happening at an accelerating exponential rate.

In 2015 Rumage and I suggested that 2050 was too far out and that 2030 should be the deadline for substantial change in how we live on the planet. This was based on this reality that Earth is showing us that it was, is, and will be warming ever more rapidly. So accept this dynamic and move the goal posts up to 2030. We both remember being told that this was "unrealistic and too radical."

In a truly significant paper published in October 2018, the UN's Intergovernmental Panel on Climate Change (IPCC) stated that incoming planetary data dictated that 2030 had to be the deadline for a massive reduction in the use of fossil fuels.

As Leonard and I wrote "Moving to a Finite Earth Economy", two things occurred. First, the research we were doing gave us both pause. We discussed whether we should even write the book as things were so much worse, so much sooner than expected. We committed to what we know to be true: everyone MUST do something, and this was our best way to do that something at a hopeful scale of impact.

Second, we made the decision that we had to lay down a timeline of action that we thought would work – the solution. Whether our ideas were immediately embraced or not, we had to at least offer a pathway forward that might be successful. Our diagnosis, prescriptive action and timeline had to be correct regardless of whether it was met or not.

"The world economy is a pyramid scheme. The world needs a new model of how to generate a rising standard of living that's not dependent on a pyramid scheme." – Steven Chu, Nobel Prize winner and the Secretary of Energy under Obama

Third, capitalism was being viewed by many as having run its course in certain ways. It has created historic levels of wealth inequality. Its fundamental drivers of creating and preserving capital depended on eternal expansion of GDP and ever growing consumption... the root causes of global warming. The touted "unicorns" created by Silicon Valley were failing investors as they went public. Prominent hedge fund managers, macroeconomists and CEOs were speaking openly about how capitalism was in dire need of reinvention.

Ironically, we felt that capitalism, unquestionably the single greatest force for material well-being in history, was a force to be leveraged if humanity has any chance of slowing, stopping and reversing climate change.

"I believe that all good things taken to an extreme can be self-destructive and that everything must evolve or die. This is now true for capitalism." – Ray Dalio, Chairman and Founder, Bridgewater Associates

Both of the above-named books are full of charts, visuals, data and timelines that will educate, shock, and open minds to a clearer understanding of what is going on. Should you want to do a deeper dive into understanding why we are approaching an irreversible planetary tipping point, please read them. This book is an introduction to this new, historically unprecedented decade. A high-level warning and prelude to what we will all be matriculating in the coming 10 years.

The 2020s is the last decade we have to alter our course relative to the planetary damage humanity has caused. We are living in a time of Anthropogenic Global Warming [AGW]. Climate change is simply the planet reacting to the warming we have created.

First, we must all stop using the phrase "Save the Planet". It is a meme that those who want to show they are environmentalists use. It is an ignorant and dangerous phrase to use. The planet doesn't need saving. Earth has been around for several billion years and will be around for several billion more until the sun explodes. Why do we think we can save the planet when it doesn't need saving?

"Save the Planet" is also a phrase that reveals the hypocrisy of many commercial enterprises who want to be on your good side. Have you ever stayed in a hotel where there is a card in the bathroom, printed in green ink, that says "Help us save the planet by hanging up the towels you will reuse." This is supposed to trigger a self-righteous act by the guest and leave an impression that the hotel cares about the planet. The true message is: we want to save time and money by not washing your towels and sheets, will you help us if we push your environmental button? It is these hypocritical messages that prevent us from really facing the task at hand.

Instead of "Save the Planet" the phrase that should be used is "We have to save ourselves from ourselves." Climate change is our ecosystem reacting to how humanity lives on the planet. We all live in Growth Economies fueled by fossil fuels. Growth Economies create waste and require consumption. Growth Economies are all based on growth. Endless, unlimited growth.

"Anyone who believes exponential growth can go on forever in a finite world is either a madman or an economist." – Kenneth Boulding (economist)

How can the vast majority of 7.8 billion humans living in Growth Economies square with the reality that we live on a finite planet? We measure health and well-being with a growth metric – GDP. Endless growth on a finite planet is insanity. Lemmings rushing ignorantly to the cliff and the end of civilization as we know it.

The other reason that "Saving ourselves from ourselves" is the right way to speak about our current climate reality is that, since we caused the problem, we must provide the solutions. Our climate crisis is something we can successfully address. If we created the problem, then we have the ability to solve it.

The Three Things We Must Do to Successfully Face Climate Change

1. Reduce the 77% of energy the world uses that is from fossil fuels in 2020 to 30% by 2030.

2. Reduce, drawdown and capture as much of the 500 gigatons we have put into the atmosphere since 1980 as we can by 2030.

3. Develop crew consciousness in as many humans as possible, as soon as possible. Hopefully two to three billion people by 2030.

Reduce the use of fossil fuels by 2030

Fossil fuels create greenhouse gas emissions (GHG). These emissions go into the atmosphere and prevent heat from escaping, thus creating a warming of our ecosphere. We have known this for decades. And it has been confirmed by measurable increases in temperature.

Since the 2015 Paris Accord, emissions were supposed to drop. They have not. Our GHG emissions have increased every year since then. Talk, concern, the wringing of hands, the flowing into the streets to demonstrate, are all increasing, but so are emissions. Humanity fiddles while Earth burns.

Global GHG emissions in 2019 was 43 gigatons. This was up more than six gigatons over 2018. We are failing in our first critical area of action.

Reduce, Drawdown, Capture 500 gigatons of resident CO^2

Before the Industrial Age, there was an estimated 730 gigatons of CO^2 in the atmosphere. We crossed 800 around 1970 and 830 in 1980. It was in 1980 that the planet started its warming trend. Today our atmosphere holds 1300 gigatons of CO^2. So the increase in resident CO^2 in the atmosphere is congruent with the warming. Simply stated, we are a 730 gigaton species living in a 1300 gigaton world.

We must clean the atmosphere from sea level up to 30,000 feet. This capture, this atmospheric cleansing is above and beyond the carbon capture at the place of origin (capturing new emissions). Currently, the cost is in the trillions of dollars to even get partially there. We must begin. We must create new technologies of atmospheric cleansing ASAP. This literally is a civilization saving technology. This means that laboratories all around the world, the innovation capitol of the planet, Silicon Valley and any place else must apply all efforts to this endeavor. How rich might someone become if they invent and deploy a technology that saves civilization?

We must begin to scale all such efforts from the lab to the atmosphere. By 2030.

Creating Crew Consciousness

"We are not going to be able to operate our Spaceship Earth successfully, nor for much longer, unless we see it as a whole spaceship and our fate as common. It has to be everybody or nobody." – R. Buckminster Fuller

"There are no passengers on Spaceship Earth. We are all crew." – Marshall McLuhan

In 1969 Fuller published "Operating Manual for Spaceship Earth". He wrote that we should regard Earth as a spaceship, but it came with no operating manual. He suggested that humanity had to immediately come up with an operating manual based upon systems thinking, because our planet is a single, incredibly complex system. And that if we didn't, we would reach a fork in the road with two paths: utopia or oblivion. We have passed the fork in the road and are hurtling down the path to oblivion.

Around the time of the first Earth Day in 1970, McLuhan picked up on Fuller's metaphor and made the statement above. For what we must now do in the 2020s, it is the single most important statement to adhere to. For too long we have been simply mindless passengers on the only spaceship we have. Because it is a planetary spaceship with finite resources, with no resupply ship coming, we must all act as crew.

So what is crew consciousness?

It is taking on crew responsibilities with a new consciousness that infuses one's actions. This is difficult to do because we have all been trained to act as passive passengers on Spaceship… to just consume mindlessly… to buy, use, discard and repeat with no thought to the consequences. Another way of stating this is that we operate in a paradigm of siloed thinking.

Siloed thinking is simply thinking and living in a silo. Our silo is consumption. We don't know the consequences of our consumption. For example did you know that:

- eating a quarter pound beef hamburger at a restaurant results in six pounds of CO^2 being released into the atmosphere?

- that the "average" American produces 16 tons of GHG emissions every year (four times the global average)?

- that manufacturing a single T-shirt (from cotton field to store shelf) requires 1,700 liters of water?

- that when the garbage is picked up from your house, it doesn't go away but is simply moved to somewhere else on Spaceship Earth?

A simple example of moving from a price-based consumer to a crew conscious non-consumer is the monthly electric bill. In dozens of speeches I have asked an audience member how much their monthly electric bill is. They always know the amount. Then when I ask them how much energy was used, they don't know. This happens every time, even when I spoke to scientists at NASA.

ThisSpaceShipEarth.org created the 2% solution. The average American home has an electric bill of ap-proximately $100 per month. This pays for about 1,000 kwh of electricity. In the vast majority of homes, this electricity is generated from fossil fuels. With 1,000 as the baseline, acting as crew means reducing that number 2% a month. So the first month you drop the kwh to 980. The second month to 960. Do that for six months and you will be at 880 kwh a month. It's easy to do if you are mindful of the energy you are using – turn out lights, unplug charging cords and electric appliances when not in use, lower the thermostat in the winter and raise it in the summer.

As you begin acting as crew, you plant seeds (without uttering a word) in the people around you. Many will adopt your behavior, creating an ever-larger group of crew members on Spaceship Earth.

When it comes to climate change, people are constantly asking, "Does what I do make a difference?" The answer is Yes! if the action is scaled up as thousands, millions and billions of people become crew members.

We know that industrialized farming, particularly the raising of beef cattle, is the largest single sector source of GHG emissions. The average American consumes 57 pounds of beef a year. What if one million people cut their beef consumption by 75%? What if 100 million people in the United States, cut their beef consumption? 100 million times 42.75 pounds (75%) equals 4.27 billion pounds. This represents 17% percent of annual worldwide beef consumption. That is a significant reduction in GHG emissions due to people acting together to crew Spaceship Earth.

Crew consciousness, evolving from passive passenger on cruise ship Earth to active crew member on Spaceship Earth, can make a huge reduction in fossil fuel use.

This awareness of scaling individual action is necessary to change markets and to buy time as humanity works with urgency to transition from blind consumption to conscious non-consumption.

A crew member will buy used whenever possible. A used car rather than a new car. A used article of clothing. A used book. Buying used means that one's buying behavior is not adversely affecting Spaceship Earth. Anything that is 'new" means that to some degree a finite resource of the planet has been expended.

So, crew consciousness, scaled up to millions can alter markets, lower GHG emissions, support business models that sell used or have any other energy reduction focus.

Crew members inevitably move to conscious non-consumption.

There is much information available online on how to change the way one acts to lower GHG emissions. Here is a page from ThisSpaceshipEarth.Org:
https://thisspaceshipearth.org/get-involved/acting-as-crew/

The key thing is that crew consciousness must spread quickly to a global critical mass to lower emissions and consumption. This must be done with URGENCY!

The 2020s is our last chance to take large, bold steps to move to a Finite Earth Economy. Not doing so means that civilization as we know it will end by the latter half of the 21st century.

The 2020s is the last decade we have to successfully address our climate crisis.

Chapter 7 - The Reinvention of Capitalism

Capitalism, the single most powerful force for the material betterment of humanity in history, will be significantly reinvented in the 2020s.

"Although I have made a fortune in the financial markets, I now fear that the untrammeled intensification of laissez-faire capitalism and the spread of market values into all areas of life is endangering our open and democratic society. The main enemy of the open society, I believe, is no longer the communist but the capitalist threat." – George Soros, legendary investor

It is clear that Capitalism needs to be reinvented… the concept is 240 years old. Adam Smith published "The Wealth of Nations" in 1776 with the observation that capitalism, not mercantilism, was the best way forward for nations. What struck me several years ago, when scanning through this towering book, was that Adam Smith died in 1792, so he never saw the blossoming of the Industrial Revolution. Think about that! The "father of capitalism" never saw the Industrial Age!

When Smith published the book, the world was still in the Agricultural Age, so his reference points were all connected to that reality. Since then there has been unprecedented growth during the production-based Industrial Age, the technology-based Information Age, and the reality altering disruptions of the Shift Age.

The practice of Capitalism, the grounded thinking about it, is always looking backward. What do economists do except to analyze data from this moment backwards to then shape their theories and forecasts. [It is a fun joke among professional futurists that if you want inaccurate forecasts, invite an economist to speak]. So, in the 2020s, a major, overwhelmingly massive effort will be, must be the reinvention of Capitalism into its new 21st century manifestation.

Our late-stage Capitalism of today is faltering. Wealth inequality is at record highs globally. The Common Good is not being addressed nor enhanced. The linear nature of Growth Economies creates ever more waste in an ecologically challenged planet. The goal of ever more growth, of growth as the only measurement of societal success, is now clearly at odds with the ecosystem of a finite planet.

"I believe that all good things taken to an extreme can be self-destructive and that everything must evolve or die. This is now true for capitalism." — Ray Dalio, Chairman and Founder, Bridgewater Associates

The Industrial Age production economy gave way to the financial economy of the Information Age. In this last part of the Shift Age, the symptoms of decay and dysfunction of Capitalism are glaring. The dynamics of the Shift Age will bring sweeping change to Capitalism.

This coming reinvention requires that we move beyond legacy thinking. Accepted economic viewpoints from the past no longer reflect the reality we are living in. The reinvention of

Capitalism, to better serve humanity and all our fellow inhabitants of Spaceship Earth, will be the most significant change agent of the 2020s. The redeployment of capitalism to better face 21st issues will be critical to our quality of life in the 2030s.

In Chapter 6, I discussed how Growth Economies are a root cause of climate change, due to their relentless need for growth on a finite planet.

"The world economy is a pyramid scheme. The world needs a new model of how to generate a rising standard of living that's not dependent on a pyramid scheme." – Steven Chu, Nobel Prize winner, Secretary of Energy under Obama

One of the central themes of "Moving to a Finite Earth Economy" is that Growth Economies, and the way they are fueled, cause climate change. Growth Economies are only measured in terms of growth. They emit ever more greenhouse gases, use ever more of Earth's resources and create ever growing streams of waste. Therefore, moving from Growth Economies to Finite Earth Economies, which do not have growth at their core, is essential.

In the book, we suggested several ways that Capitalism could be an effective force in addressing our climate crisis. A key component is to change the metrics of taxation. Currently in the United States, and most other countries, taxation is based on income. We suggested replacing income taxes with carbon footprint taxes. Income is a good thing. It is a measurement of success, that one has a high income. So we currently tax something we all think is good, which is why there is so much time and effort spent on finding ways to reduce individual and corporate tax burdens.

Taxing carbon emissions would quickly reduce those emissions. It makes sense to tax what is bad rather than what is good. A classic cases of taxation to discourage a behavior is tobacco. The Surgeon General's report in 1964 confirming that tobacco causes cancer triggered a national conversation and started a slow decline of cigarette purchases. But it wasn't until significant increases in the taxation of tobacco products in the 1970s that dramatic reductions in use were achieved.

"We should no longer measure our wealth and success in the graph that shows economic growth, but in the curve that shows the emissions of greenhouse gases. We should no longer only ask: 'Have we got enough money to go through with this?' but also, 'Have we got enough carbon budget to spare to go through with this?' That should and must become the center of our new currency." — Greta Thunberg, Swedish climate change activist

Decreasing carbon emissions is the first action we must take. So, let's tax it. The average American is responsible for roughly 16 tons of carbon emissions every year. The global average, including the United States is four tons. So, in the United States there could be a new tax code that only taxes emissions, and we should begin that taxation at the fifth ton. My mathematical calculations suggest that, depending on the tax rate applied, tax revenues might be significantly higher than current revenues. It also, at least initially, would be more equitable as those who own multiple houses and cars, and travel frequently by air would pay substantially greater taxes. Therefore, a carbon emissions-based tax code would also be a big step forward in addressing global wealth inequality.

Those at the high end of emissions would want to lower taxes and could do so by taking steps most beneficial in addressing our climate crisis: buying an electric vehicle, installing solar panels, buying carbon offsets, and investing in technologies in the carbon capture industry are just a few examples. Simply by tinkering with the tax code, emissions would be lowered.

"The capitalist beast is out of control. I have a very low opinion of capitalism in 2019. We have reached a low point. The greatest manifestation of that is the massive emphasis on maximizing short-term profits, which is simply bad business. It is incredibly bad for society, and it's not good for long-term growth rates. It tends to give you better short-term profit margins and lower economic growth. For capitalism to work, you need there to be some sense of social contract – social discipline, if you will." – Jeremy Grantham, Investment Strategist

During the Transformation Decade there were many new ideas bubbling up about Capitalism. The idea for corporations to commit to the common good came into being. The Conscious Capitalism movement began. The effort to have corporations move from short-term profits only concerned with the welfare of shareholders began to evolve to a longer-term view of considering the welfare of all stakeholders (shareholders, customers, suppliers, employees, community, etc.).

The environmental community began to insist that the value of the natural world be accounted for... to include natural resources in the balance sheets of corporations. This would account for the use of precious and declining resources in our over-populated over-stressed planet.

All of these efforts are simply current thinking which reflects current realities. Capitalism has proven its vitality and adaptability throughout its history. It is now time for it to be recast to face and help solve the civilization threatening risks of this century.

More wealth has been created between 1900 and today than was created in the sum total of all prior years. That is the power of Capitalism. Let's take that power and redeploy it to address the existential threats to humanity and to our ecosphere that we are experiencing in the 2020s.

The 2020s, due to the magnitude of disruption and the multiple forks in the road we face, is truly the decade that will dictate the trajectory of humanity at least through 2050, if not longer. This means that all known useful, influential and powerful forces must be aligned with this need to put the long-,term well-being of humanity and all living things in place.

What do we know about Capitalism? That it is the most powerful force for the creation of material well-being in history. It shapes how we think about all things economic, from the micro focus on making and saving money to the macro focus on national economies and the global economy.

In the 2020s, as the Shift Age brings its' last massive dose of disruption, transformational needs and threats to a close, one of the key points is to update Capitalism to the realities of this decade. Remember it was created in the Agricultural Age when land determined wealth. It massively defined itself and thrived in the Industrial Age of production in the 1800s and 1900s. It "won" the "war" against Communism. The American way of life "triumphed" and we all became consumers.

It no longer works when viewed through the lens of the climate crisis, the coming transformation of Technological Intelligence, the massive global debt overhang as we enter the decade, and the explosion of wealth inequality. Capitalism has in fact become well-oiled plutocracies in many places of the world. It no longer fulfills the promise that American Democracy; to "be for the people, by the people, of the people".

Perhaps the highest level of reality and flow dynamics, reinventing Capitalism to be aligned with the 2020s and the 21st Century is essential. Think of the reinvention as central to the curriculum we must matriculate if we are to have a future of abundance, evolving civilization and to prepare for our next evolutionary next step.

A tall order but an essential one for the 2020s.

Chapter 8 – The 21st Century Democracy

"Our Age of Anxiety is, in great part, the result of trying to do today's job with yesterday's tools and yesterday's concepts." – Marshall McLuhan

A much overdue reinvention and recalibration of Democracy will occur during the 2020s. Democracy is the most desirable form of government, but it has become dysfunctional… corrupted by money, supportive of a plutocracy and run on stale, no longer valid ideas.

Autocratic regimes are on the rise and democracies are failing. The threat to democracies in the 21st Century is much more from within than without.

Democracy and Capitalism are closely tied as democracies are capitalistic and capitalism best thrives under democracy. In the prior chapter we discussed the failing of late stage Capitalism. The same could be said of late stage Democracy.

Democracy came into being at the end of the 18th century with the French and American revolutions. It has endured more than 200 years and it has undergone many changes. Initially in America, only male landowners had the right to vote. Then men who didn't own land were allowed to vote; then women; then black men and women. Ever more universal voting rights.

The fact that the great American Democratic experiment survives to this day is proof that it is flexible, adaptive and remarkable. Now however, voting rights are challenged, gerrymandering protects political parties, foreign governments and bad actors are hacking elections, social media has created mistrust and misguidance and voter turnout is low. In other words the participation in the single most important function of democracies – elections- is being challenged.

However, its remarkability is in question in this new century. It is difficult to find a Democracy that has not, to some extent, been corrupted by money. This is of concern, as Thomas Jefferson warned:

"The end of Democracy and the defeat of the American Revolution will occur when government falls into the hands of lending institutions and moneyed incorporations." – Thomas Jefferson

Are we at the end of Democracy? No, but we are in need of deep changes. Banks triggered the Great Recession of 2008 - 2012 and corporations control much of the lobbying efforts today in the United States.

Around the world, money and Capitalism have eaten Democracy for lunch. Lobbyists now seem to be as much a force in legislation as anything else. Vast sums of money are spent to influence legislators at all levels of government. Campaign contributions, gifts, and constant lobbying have greater influence than the desires and welfare of the voting public. The largest amount of money spent on lobbyists in the United States comes from corporations.[1] Was this envisioned by the founding fathers of the United States or the founders of democracies elsewhere in the world?

There are several ways that this financial influence could be altered in this decade. First, there could be a federal/state/local level of public funding of elections. Long discussed in the United States, but never given much of a chance to be implemented. Those of the monied status quo have successfully resisted the idea. Second, the entire representation structure could change. While radical, this is worth consideration.

To use my native United States as the example, our current ways of voting are based on historical legacy thinking. At the end of the 18th century and through the 19th century, information moved slowly. Communication was by letter, so it took days. The solution in this Agricultural Age economy was to set up a representational form of government. This allowed elected officials to be in Washington D.C. (or state capitals) to represent their constituents at a distance.

Today zettabytes of data move at the speed of light through fiber optic cables. We know instantly what is happening anywhere in the world. Remote, physical representation does not make sense in an ever more connected world.

[1] https://www.opensecrets.org/news/2019/01/lobbying-spending-reaches-3-4-billion-in-18/

The technologies of the 21st century are woefully lacking in the functioning of government, certainly relative to the interaction between voter and legislators, and even within the functioning of Congress. The Senate rules dictate that a Senator cannot vote if they cannot make it to the chamber floor. Why penalize the citizens from that state? Why not accept a vote from a Senator via video conferencing?

An idea suggested in a white paper by The Sarasota Institute in 2018 (disclaimer: I am a Co-Founder and Managing Director of this 21st Century Think Tank) is to have the electorate not vote for representative candidates based upon political party, but upon issues and knowledge of issues. People are concerned about issues that affect them. People vote on issues as much as they vote by party. This is why Independents are now a larger group than either of the two political parties in the United States.

"We believe it is time for technology to disintermediate politicians and political parties. Importantly, all of this is currently possible technologically-speaking. What is wanting is the will power to engage in a dialogue to initiate democracy into the 21st Century." –
The Sarasota Institute Whitepaper (Big Issues - #1)

So the electorate could vote for policy experts instead of partisan party politicians. Or not. Either way the understanding would be that the winning candidate, policy savvy, would commit to letting her constituency vote via technology to shape policy for the elected representative. Once legislation is in formative stages, these policy rep-resentatives could reach out to their constituents to allow them to "vote" via technology on it. This acknowledges that 21st century technology exists and can be used to create a direct form of representation, rather than the current one step removed representational democracy that is based upon lobbyists and no term limits. In addition, most if not all legislation is created by staffers of the office holder. The people, when they vote, have no idea who the staffers will be and what their expertise is. The power would remain with the people rather than be offloaded to career politicians and political parties.

In the same whitepaper, The Sarasota Institute suggested a way to avoid the experience every reader of this book has experienced: voting for "the lesser of two evils" In addition to the candidate for the Republican Party and the candidate for the Democratic Party, there would be a third option: none of the above. In this case if "none of the above" won, the two parties would have to put up other candidates up until one of them won the approval of the voters for whom they will work

With regard to candidates, regardless of the overall popularity of those competing for office, someone will get elected because there is no way to vote "no" on all of the candidates. The long stated frustration of voting for "lesser of two evils" – a direct result of the two-party duopoly in the U.S. for example – will be addressed by allowing voters to show their frustration with an out-of-date party system that forces the two candidates to be against each other rather have unique policy positions. This makes voting more of what it really is: a job interview conducted by the citizens.

"There is nothing which I dread so much as a division of the republic into two great parties, each arranged under its leader, and concerting measures in opposition to each other. This, in my humble apprehension, is to be dreaded as the greatest political evil under our Constitution." – John Adams

In the American Democracy, Congress in general and the Senate in particular, operate not under antiquated rules, but with a speed slower than all other aspects of the society they represent. This will no longer work in the 2020s.

The eminent futurists, Alvin and Heidi Toffler, in their book *Revolutionary Wealth,* commented on the relative speeds with which social institutions change. First, they suggest the metaphor of a motorcycle cop sitting on the side of a highway pointing his radar gun at the oncoming traffic. "On the highway there are nine cars, each representing a major institution in America. Each car travels at a speed that matches that institution's actual rate of change." They then go on to list, from fastest to slowest:

100 mph	Corporations
90 mph	Civil society including NGOs
60 mph	The American Family
30 mph	Unions
25 mph	Government bureaucracies and regulatory agencies
10 mph	The American school system
5 mph	International or intergovernmental agencies
3 mph	Political structures in developed countries – Congress, the Presidency, political parties
1 mph	The Law

This metaphor brings such clarity to so much of the tensions and battles in America. Obviously, companies moving at 100 mph change will have a hard time with regulatory agencies who move at 25. Critical global problems cannot be addressed by intergovernmental agencies, such as the WTO, the World Bank or any of the global institutions created decades ago in a post-WWII world.

The key point here is the extremely slow rate of change of Congress, the Presidency and the [current] two political parties.

As the Tofflers wrote in 2006:

"Can a hyperspeed, twenty-first-century info-biological economy continue to advance? Or will society's slow-paced, malfunctioning, obsolete institutions grind its progress to a halt?"[2]

A rhetorical question in 2006 is now a critical issue as we enter the 2020s. By now the reader should have grasped the underlying theme of this book: prepare for a decade of unprecedented disruption and massive changes.

Democracy must change. It must update itself to match the world around it, or it will die an arteriosclerotic death, clinging to the traditions of an Agricultural Age world.

[2] "Revolutionary Wealth", Alvin and Heidi Toffler, Alfred A. Knopf, 2006

Ideas to Consider

American Democracy is, by definition, *"of the people, by the people, for the people."* Elections are the base line. Beyond elections there will need to be some fundamental updating of the structures, processes and functions of Democracy in America. Ideas must be delivered to the public commons for consideration.

Integration of current technologies can and should be implemented. A clear example of this is Estonia, which has not only digitized most aspects of government, but is perhaps the only country in the world where the coolest place to work IS the government. An employer of first choice rather than last resort. However, Estonia is smaller than many states, so it's success should be studied to determine if they can scale.

In the aforementioned white paper from The Sarasota Institute, there were two ideas put forth that address the realities of American Democracy in this century.

One idea set forth in this white paper is to eliminate the current practice of each party putting forth candidates for President and Vice-President. Negative campaigning, smear campaigns, and high partisanship is a current consequence of this practice. Instead, the idea would be that each party would put up only a candidate for President and that these two candidates would campaign on the concept of being the better person to lead the country for the next four years. The winner becomes the President and the loser becomes Vice-President. Negative campaigning and partisanship would drop dramatically as the winner and the loser would have to work together for four years.

Article 2 Section 1 of the U.S. Constitution stipulates that the President and Vice-President must be elected every four years.

It does not stipulate that these two must be from the same party.

Radical idea? Not really, just different from our 20th century thinking.

So, the integration of technology into all processes of government, the "none of the above" option for voters, and two presidential candidates competing to be President with the loser becoming VP, are just three of many potential ways to update and improve the American Democracy.

As a futurist, I am not so concerned about which specific new policies, procedures and changes to elections are implemented, as I am about the clear need for democracies around the world to drop 19th and 20th century traditions that no longer serve the citizens.

A good place to start would be to ask this question:

"What should Democracies look like in the 21st Century?

What is ahead in the 2020s requires we answer this question... ASAP!

Chapter 9 - The Next Evolutionary Leap

In the 2020s we will start to see what the probable next step of our human evolutionary path could be. This, in large part, depends upon how we, humanity, navigate and collaborate in the next ten years.

To again reference the fork in the road mentioned in the early part of this book:

"In several decades, humanity will be at a fork in the road: utopia or oblivion. Either a utopia of abundance or an oblivion of destruction." –
R. Buckminster Fuller, 1969

As a futurist, I have always stated that I reverentially stand on the shoulders of the three greatest futurists of the last 70 years: Buckminster Fuller, Marshall McLuhan and Alvin Toffler to look ahead into the 21st century. Fuller's quote was within the context of the need to address looming global issues (poverty, climate, social justice, over-population) with global systems thinking. Of course, humanity has not done so, which is why his words are still important as we enter the 2020s. We need to approach these extremely complex and interconnected problems with urgency and collaborative systems thinking.

"The new electronic independence re-creates the world in the image of a global village." – Marshall McLuhan

We have entered the global stage of human evolution. There is no turning back. The nationalistic and siloed thinking of the past will not work to solve global problems anymore. They are, in fact, often the causes of our present global issues and threats.

During the 2020s, humanity will fully realize that we are at a new, global stage of the evolution of our species. How this realization is collectively manifested will be a major story line of these next ten years.

So where are we now, in 2020?

Simply put, in terms of standard social and economic measurements, humanity is now at the apotheosis of our evolutionary journey. Steven Pinker, in his magnificent book "Enlightenment Now" documented this case. In the last 200 years, humanity has, generally:

- created more wealth than in all of history prior to 1800

- doubled life expectancy

- reduced extreme poverty from 90% to 10%

- tripled the level of education

- dramatically lowered deaths due to famine.

In many basic issues, we are doing well, and it happened concurrently with an increase in population from one billion to 7.8 billion. So these achievements are truly impressive. However, this 780% increase in population is now causing significant stress in most areas of human endeavor. The Earth hasn't grown, nor have the amount of natural resources.

Thinking into the rest of this century, how we view population growth and over population will be critical. Unlimited population growth on a finite planet is lunacy. Population planning, at a national and global level, will be crucial in the 2020s. This far transcends the issues around abortion and religious dogma (is there any religion that addresses population in any way other than to promote increasing the number of followers?) This is at the core of whether we can collectively move into systems planning at a species level.

The big issues of population management, wealth equality, decent living conditions, global migrations, global warming, public health challenges and access to our ever more electronically connected global human reality must all be viewed in new ways if we are to avoid Fuller's path to Oblivion.

Machiavelli's statement was true when he wrote it in "The Prince" and it is still true today:

"There is nothing more difficult to plan, more uncertain of success, nor dangerous to manage than the creation of a new order of things. For the initiator has the enmity of all those who would profit by the preservation of the old institutions, and merely lukewarm defenders in those who would gain by the new ones."

The single greatest threat to our next evolutionary step is insisting on holding onto the legacy thinking of the past. As someone who has glimpsed the future and moved towards it, I have suffered many arrows in my back, from those who refuse to let go of the status quo. The quote that has given me solace, and is key for all of us in the 2020s, is from the great philosopher Schopenhauer:

"In the revelation of any truth there are three stages. In the first it is ridiculed. In the second it is resisted. In the third it is considered self-evident."

Think back. The sun revolves around the earth. The earth is flat. Climate change isn't real. All of these notions have progressed through these three stages.

The 2020s will bring us, haltingly, to self-evident realizations in many areas. Whether we embrace these realizations and make them manifest will be the deciding factor.

So we now stand at the apotheosis of human evolution. We have elevated the quality of life for more people in the last 200 years in unprecedented ways. The fork in the road is real. The path toward oblivion is to not change, to not successfully address our climate crisis, to not progress from nationalism to a global stage of human evolution.

So what does the road to utopia look like? What does the road to abundance look like? What will our next evolutionary step look like?

Our Possible Next Evolutionary Step

Darwin, the father of evolution, published "The Origin of Species" in 1859. It was transformational because it challenged the religious myths that had shaped our sense of our world. It is arguably one of the most significant books ever published.

In it Darwin, a biologist, suggested that man's evolutionary journey had accelerated due to developments including the establishment of agriculture, language, society, government and the marketplace. Subsequent Darwin followers, steeped in the new field of anthropology, solidified this view.

In the 160 years since the publication of "The Origin of Species", we know that humans are taller, heavier and live much longer. While it has been proclaimed by thinkers such as Stephen J. Gould that there hasn't been any biological change to humans for tens of thousands of years[1], how we live in our built environments has profoundly changed.

Culturally and socially there have been massive changes: electricity and all the inventions that have flowed from it, public schooling, flight, electronic media, and massive amounts of information available at any time to billions of humans.

All of these things have brought rapid changes to how we live, how we spend our time and how we interact with each other. Theoretically, this radical altering and upgrading of human environments suggest that we have evolved almost as much since 1859 as humans did the 5,000 years prior, if not biologically, most certainly in many other ways.

[1] http://www.capitalideasonline.com/wordpress/good-read/the-spice-of-life-an-interview-with-stephen-jay-gould/

The vision I hold for our next step of human evolution is a simple but hard to imagine. We are in the global stage of human evolution. We are becoming ever more reliant and aligned with technology. If we successfully deal with the climate crisis and are successful in reinventing Capitalism and Democracy in the 2020s, we might evolve as much by 2050 as we have evolved since 1869 and equal to the 5,000 years before that.

Since "Origin" was published, many scientists have de-livered a more modern interpretation of Darwin's writing. A professor, W.C. Allee, expressed it well:

"The sub-social and social life of animals shows two major tendencies: one toward aggressiveness, which is best developed in man and his fellow vertebrates; the other towards unconscious, and in higher animals, toward conscious cooperation. With various associates I have long experimented upon both tendencies. Of these, the drive toward cooperation… is the more elusive and the more important."[2]

In the 2020s, humanity needs to advance toward this elusive tendency, which pairs up nicely with the essential adoption of systems thinking. To continue upward on our evolutionary journey, we will need to embrace cooperation and move away from aggression. Our aggressive tendencies must now be collectively directed toward solving the aforementioned global problems.

[2] Darwin's Century, Loren Eiseley, Anchor Books, 1961

If humanity successfully addresses the challenges listed in Chapter 3, the path to abundance and utopia could be our next evolutionary step over the next three to four decades.

As suggested in Chapter 5, we have entered the Age of Intelligence. This means that the merger or blending of Human and Technological Intelligence will be our next evolutionary step. A constant theme in science fiction is the blending of humanity with TI or robots. This could become science fact in the second half of the 2020s. Look at the technology today compared to 15 years ago. Smart phones, cloud computing, online everything and the global reality of no time, distance or place any longer limiting human communications didn't exist prior to the Shift Age.

The Progression

We are clearly moving to a human/technology integration. What that might ultimately look like? The degree of symbiosis and benevolence is yet to be determined. It will happen. Take a look at this high-level progression of man's integration of technology.

Modern Humanity has been on the planet for 150,000 years. 170 years ago, the telegraph was invented and widely deployed. It's only been 1/10,000 of 1% of our time on the planet that we been able to communicate without being face to face. Since then technology has become an integral part of our lives.

Progression

Telegraph – created place to place communication.

Electricity – provides the energy for technologies going forward.

Radio – the ear to the world (one way).

Telephone – person to person communication (bi-directional).

Television – window to the world (one way).

Proliferation

One radio per household to three+ per household

One telephone per household to two+ per household

One TV per household to two+ per household

Marshall McLuhan, in "The Medium is the Message", wrote the simple truth about the electronic village, TV in particular. The fact that say 60 million people were watching TV at one time is a much more significant, than what they were watching. The Global Village was created by TV and satellite broadcast.

Cable television delivered programming niched by demographics – something for everyone.

The Internet delivered global multi-channel omni-directional connectivity and communication.

The Smart Phone supplies a powerful, multi-functional hand-held computer that creates a 'no time, distance or place' reality of human communication.

The chart below shows how, since 1900 adoption rates and market penetration of technology has sped up. The telephone took 100 years to get to market saturation. The TV took 30 years. The PC took 20 years. The cell phone, digital camera and Internet took 10 years. The smart phone, HDTV and the tablet took 3 years.

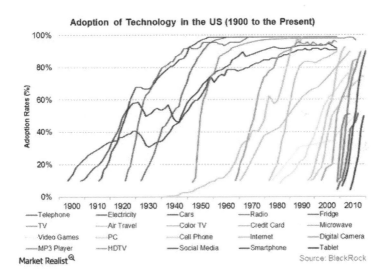

So what we see is that in the first full century of technology for humanity, the integration and market saturation of technology is accelerating. Today is the slowest speed of technological change you will experience in your lifetime.

Externalization of the Brain

This began with writing. For example, we make a list of things to do tomorrow, taking this list out of our brain onto a piece of paper, so we don't have to remember it. Now we have externalized our brain further with GPS in our phones. We follow the directions of a nice sounding woman and don't need to refer to a map or landmarks. We take a picture of where we parked our car at an airport so we can find it when we return. We even have externalized the phone numbers of people close to us. (I just hit my sons' name on my iPhone, I don't know his number.) Now, with larger screen hand-held devices, we have made them our library, video viewing device, audio listening device and social interaction platform. This single device allows us to externalize our brain.

We now externalize our brains to our personal devices. We will, perhaps by 2030 be able to externalize our brains to our environments. Our office or living room will be intelligent, going beyond where we are now which is smart devices.

Direct Brain Stimulation – some 100,000 Americans now have imbedded, miniature electric devices in their brains that lessen or stop the symptoms of Parkinson's disease. That's an insertion of technology into the human body.

Smart Environments – we are living in homes equipped with smart doorbells, thermostats, and audio hubs such as Alexa. We are reinventing our living environments with technology. As mentioned above we now moving from "dumb" environments to "smart environments". By the end of the 2020s we will be living and working in intelligent environments. Ones that actually have intelligence about the room and the people in it, at least to a rudimentary degree.

This progression is clearly moving toward an ever-greater symbiosis between humans and technology. In the last 170 years, technology has moved ever more into our lives. This progression will accelerate in the 2020s. What the end of the decade reality will look like is conjecture at this time, but from the vantage point of 2030, we will look back at 2020 as an elemental stage of human/technology integration

"The next major explosion is going to be when genetics and computers come together. I'm talking about an organic computer... about biological substances that can function like a semiconductor." – Alvin Toffler

Within a few years, some humans will have memory chips imbedded in their brains. Think of this as a possible technological cure for Alzheimer's. Artificial joints are commonplace surgeries. 3-D printing of body parts for technology-enhanced hearing and sight are not far off. By the end of the 2020s we may well have to revisit the definition of life as we have accepted it up to now.

"One of the more fantastic possibilities is that man will be able to make biological carbon copies of himself." – Alvin Toffler

The real ascendant merger is when TI replaces much of our repetitive work, first in developed countries, then globally. This will unleash the greatest amount of human potential in history. Humans can become ever more human: free to be creative while technology performs the drudgery. Humans can deploy systems thinking toward the common good, environmental restoration, and address our other societal issues.

This should be our vision as we embark on the road to Utopia.

It will closely track a new global consciousness and sense of self.

Chapter 10 – Consciousness and the Self

Closely tied to the next evolutionary step for humanity is the move to a global consciousness and how that affects the new split sense of self.

I began my career as a futurist 15 years ago in 2006. My first flag in the ground was my blog titled "EvolutionShift" with the subtitle "A Future Look at Today".

The reason I used this name was that even back then it was clear to me that the new age we were entering was a transit to an evolutionary shift of consciousness. The Shift Age was in part named that to reflect this vision: the age when we shifted our consciousness from the pre-year 2000 sense of self to a new accelerating global consciousness in the 21st century.

In "The Shift Age" which was published in 2007, I wrote:

- *Tools defined the Agricultural Age*

- *Machines defined the Industrial Age*

- *Technology defined the Information Age*

- *Consciousness will define the Shift Age*

Consciousness is one of those words that has a number of definitions, and is also at the root of many medical, philosophical, religious and metaphysical treatises. It also forms the core of one's sense of self. What I saw clearly 14 years ago was that humanity would experience both a collective and an individual altering of consciousness; and would develop a dual sense of self in the first decades of the 21st century.

What are the trends and dynamics of this shift?

Technology and Connectivity

The iPhone first came to market in 2007. Same with the Kindle. The number of total cell phones in use has grown 1700% between 2000 and 2020.[1]

In 2020, the total number of people who have cell phones is 5.28 billion which is 68% of humanity. Since 2005, the speed of connectivity has increased dramatically – from 2G to 4G and soon to 5G. The number of people with access to the Internet has increased almost 400% between 2005 and 2019, rising from 1.1 billion to 4.2 billion people.

[1] https://qz.com/9101/mobile-phones-developing-world/

When people learn that I am a futurist, they often ask: "Oh, so you talk about the future of technology?" To which I always respond: "No I talk about how technology will change human behavior." Technology is reshaping our world, reshaping every aspect of how we live. As referenced in Chapters 5 and 9, technology is even facilitating our next evolutionary step.

There is no time, distance or place connected to communication anymore. One can be anywhere in the world and can connect to anyone else in the world, right now! This means that technology has moved us from a place-based sense of communication to a space-based one. Wireless is in the air. Communication devices are in our hands and ears.

This Place to Space dynamic is one of the larger contexts for this move to global consciousness and will be dealt with a bit later in this chapter.

Noosphere / Neurosphere

Pierre Teilhard de Chardin was both an ordained Jesuit priest and a successful paleontologist. In his most famous book "The Phenomenon of Man" he successfully reconciled his faith with the science of evolution. (Note: this great book was published post-mortem as Chardin could not publish while alive. Galileo anyone?) He argued that humanity was evolving toward a mass and intensity of thought that would ultimately create a force, a collective consciousness. He named this the Noosphere.

When I read this book in the early part of this century, it profoundly affected me. Here was a brilliant scholar who had provided a sound scientific and spiritual foundation for the vision I had that humanity was progressing toward a new global consciousness.

Starting around the time that my first book "The Shift Age" was published in 2007, I began speaking about the coming evolution shift, a shift initially driven by our ever-accelerating connectedness via technology. In a nod to Teilhard de Chardin, I named this new reality "the Neurosphere".

This Neurosphere is a pulsating, synaptic Internet-based technological model of what this new consciousness might look like. As I wrote in my 2013 book "Entering the Shift Age":

This connectedness, happening at the speed of light via fiber optics, is creating an entire new place: the Neurosphere. Our physical reality exists in the biosphere — the thin surface of the planet where life exists. But this new, rapidly growing neurosphere is the electronic extension of our collective neurological activity. It is a pulsing cyber-repository of humanity's creative brainpower, its knowledge, history, culture, social interactions, entertainment and commerce. This is a global village vastly more comprehensive and interconnected than Marshall McLuhan could ever have envisioned when he coined the phrase "global village" more than forty years ago. We now live in a two-reality world: the physical reality in which we live and the neurosphere reality of the screen that connects us to everything and everyone else on the planet.

The neurosphere has become ever faster, more inter-connected and much more visual than when I wrote those words eight years ago. In the 2020s, the neurosphere will launch us into a preliminary collective consciousness. By the end of this decade, some portion of humanity will be tapping into this new global brain of collective thought. Not that we are thinking the same thing because of the speed that data and information moves around the world, but an almost telepathic connection. We have all had that experience of thinking of calling someone we haven't spoken to in a while, and then they call us. Or being with people and someone says something, and you say, "I was just thinking that!"

"We shape our tools and afterwards our tools shape us." – Marshall McLuhan

We often speak about being connected by love, of having a connection of the heart. Many people talk about psychic connection. Our next step is consciousness and brain connection

Referencing the merging of humanity and technology in the prior chapter, there are brain-to-computer interfaces that allow one to direct a computer with thought. Yes, thought! Think of the progression so far. First there were people that had to deal with tape and punch cards to input into the mainframe computer. Then we got our own personal computers and we used disks and keyboards. Then we had touch screens. Now we use voice and sound.

By the mid-2020s many of us will be interfacing with our computers via brainwaves. Is it not fair to make the assumption that after a few years of developing the skill of brainwave-computer interface we will have the capability to connect brain to brain?

For decades this has been called Brain Machine Interface [BMI] a term from the last century when the computer was often referenced as a machine. Now we will finally realize this vision though it will be Brain Computer Interface [BCI].

A new global consciousness is one of the four overarching forces that will shape the 2020s. The Neurosphere, as it exists today in 2020, will be the technological departure point for this new phenomenon.

The last chapter of "Entering the Shift Age" was a theoretical look back from the vantage point of 2033, 20 years after the book had been published. The book ended this way:

We now see the logical merging of physical and screen realities discussed for the first time in that book. How could we live without it now? Finally the evolutionary shift in consciousness predicted in that first edition of 'Entering the Shift Age' has turned out to be so much more beautiful and meaningful than could have been imagined. The reality of the collective consciousness and awareness most of us regularly experience seems even greater than the dreams and early visions of it going back a century (Chardin). It really is becoming an evolution shift even greater than imagined. In and of itself it has altered humanity more than anything else these past twenty years. How wonderful to be alive now!

This vision may or may not be a reality in 2033. Whether it is or not will largely depend on how well we navigate the 2020s. Whether we truly take the path of utopia and abundance, or stumble down the path of destruction.

Place to Space

Humanity has, during my lifetime, shifted from a mostly place-based consciousness to an ever more space-based consciousness. This is largely due to the technology that severed the tether between human communication to place – there is no longer a time, distance or place limit to human communications.

The Interstate Highway system, created under President Eisenhower, largely ended the distinct differences of regions, states and cities. The country was homogenized as regions, states and cities lost much of their individuality. Now we see the same restaurant, gasoline, hotel and retail chains anywhere in America. It is interesting to note that the genesis of the idea for the Interstate Highway system came to Eisenhower when he led a cross-country trip from Washington to San Francisco in 1919, to show off to the country the vehicles used to win WWI.

The only cross-country highway at that time was the Lincoln Highway. It took 62 days to cross the country. When Ike became President he remembered this experience and determined that, in post-WWII America, speed was needed, and that an Interstate Highway System could provide it. Now that 62 day car trip can be done in five days. The highway system made the United States a more cohesive unit.

We all have had the experience of being on a plane when someone sits down next to you and asks: "So, where are you from?" When I answered with, "Chicago," 50% of people said, "Are you a Sox or a Cub fan?" 25% said, "Ah, the Windy City" and the last quarter said "great restaurant town.: So this became a barely tolerable, highly predictable interchange.

However, when I thought about it, I realized that it was really an insightful question. Depending upon whether a person was born in Chicago, New York, Miami, London, Mumbai or Rio, the differences were profound. You dress differently, eat differently, speak differently and root for difference teams. Humans sense of self, at least up to this century, was very much place-based. If someone said they were from New England, they were probably a Patriots, Celtics or Red Sox fan.

It used to be that when you saw the area code on an incoming phone call, you could assume that the person was actually in that location. I live in Florida now, but have kept my Chicago cell phone number. Some people, thinking that the world hasn't changed, assume I am in Chicago. Nope. I live in Florida, a state that is the home of many people who have moved here from somewhere else, so this state has millions of phone numbers from all around the country.

When I was a young boy, I knew that my aunts and uncles lived in Florida some 1,500 miles away. That meant that I got a call on my birthday and Christmas, and that every other year we drove down to visit the family. So I had a keen sense of distance and place when it came to these relatives. Today, children, from the earliest ages, regularly tap the touch screen on a phone and say hello to grandma. Grandma is here, on my screen, anytime I want to talk to her. That deconstructs any sense of place or distance. Grandma exists in space.

William Gibson gave us the term cyberspace[2]. Not cyberplace.

The speed and ubiquity of technology is the portal into this growing place that is no place, but rather space. The portal to this new space is, of course, the screen.

[2] Neuromancer, William Gibson, Ace, 1984

Generations

This decades long transfer from place to space can be seen through a generational lens and continuum. The boomers were the last generation to grow into adulthood in a place-based consciousness. We didn't play online. We played outside in the neighborhood. We did see the world beyond our neighborhood via television, but the television stations were physically local and locally oriented.

The GenX generation was a bridge generation. About half were born in a place-based consciousness and were children in the late 1960s and 1970s, but were young or not born when the Apple computer came out in 1976.

The Millennials grew up with computers and early cell phones. They were the first generation to have these devices well before their adulthood. They were the first generation to utilize email and texting as children or teenagers. They were the first generation to play both outside and online.

Digital Natives, first born in the late 1990s, is the first generation that grew up with cell phones, and had use of cell phones starting in childhood. This first generation of the 21st century is fully of this century, so analog is something they never experienced, and Wi-Fi was an accepted reality.

So this chronological arc of transition from place to space is clearly represented in the linear progression from Boomer to Digital Native, from Pen Pals to international online gaming, from cable TV to interactive wireless handheld devices, from landline phones to video chat, from local news to global news delivered instantaneously. An analog consciousness to a digital one.

The Duality of Sense of Self

There is a new historically unprecedented split developing in our sense of self. Starting with the generational lens, the Boomers grew up with a place-based sense of self. The individual. The existential hero. Alienation of the self from the larger society or culture. The cowboy or the rebel on the motorcycle riding off into the sunset. Me. Dating was the teenage norm.

Contrast that with the dominant descriptive of the Millennial generation. We. Dating or socializing in groups. Much more of a collective social sense.

The Digital Natives was the first generation to grow up with social media, which of course is a shared, collective experience. Two selves were created… the in-person person and the online person. A bifurcation of the developing sense of self.

Now fold in the reality of managing screen and physical realities. This is me in physical place and this is me in cyberspace. Layer over this the reality that we have entered the global stage of human evolution and this duality of self becomes viewable in the macro-arc of history. Remember the three dominant flows of the Shift Age: the flow to global, the flow to the individual, and the accelerating connectedness of humanity. So we are increasingly individuals connected globally. We have an ever more global sense of self.

This global consciousness is now being amplified by our climate crisis. As we realize the finite limitations of Spaceship Earth, we (especially the young) no longer view ourselves as individual passengers. We are crew members on Spaceship

Earth. The reality of our climate crisis is that now, all living things have the same common enemy: how humanity lives on Spaceship Earth. We are developing a unified sense that all of us are the collective solution. Remember that developing "crew consciousness" was one of the three things humanity has to do to face climate change.

This duality of self will continue to grow through the 2020s. It is in fact the precursor to the coming integration of technological intelligence and humanity... our next evolutionary step.

The 2020s will shape and accelerate this duality of self in ways that will be part of the unprecedented creative destruction ahead.

Postscript

This is the first book of a series with the overarching title "the 2020s" This book sets the stage for the books that will follow. These books will be much more subject specific.

This book did not take you long to read, right? That is the idea, to write and publish a series of short books. Increasingly we all live in an ever shorter-attention span world. My limited research confirms that people shy away from multi-hundred page non-fiction books.

The goal here is to have this be a series of short (100 pages or less) that are subject specific relative to different significant developments of the 2020s. They will be priced accordingly I promise.

Here is a tentative list of titles, sequence not yet firm.

The 2020s: Decade of Cognitive Dissonance

The 2020s: The Golden Age of Design and Redesign

The 2020s: Financial Disruption or Collapse?

The 2020s: The New Planetary Reality

The 2020s: The New Geo-Political Landscape

The 2020s: The Age of Intelligence

The 2020s: A New Consciousness

The 2020s: Evolutionary Acceleration

Biography

David Houle is a futurist, speaker and strategist. Houle spent more than 20 years in Media and Entertainment. He worked at NBC, CBS and was part of the senior executive team that created and launched MTV, Nickelodeon, VH-1 and CNN Headline News.

Houle has won a number of awards. He won two Emmys, the prestigious George Foster Peabody Award and the Heartland Award for "Hank Aaron: Chasing the Dream". He was also nominated for an Academy Award. He is the Futurist in Residence at the Ringling College of Art + Design, the Co-Founder and Managing Director of The Sarasota Institute – A 21st Century Think Tank, and the Honorary Futurist at the Future Business School of China.

He has delivered 1000+ speeches, presentations, and corporate retreats on six continents and in sixteen countries. He is often called "the CEO's Futurist" having spoken to or advised 4,500+ CEOs and business owners in the past eleven years. He presented "This Spaceship Earth" to scientists at the NASA Goddard Space Flight Center and at the EPA.

Houle coined the phrase the Shift Age and has written extensively about the future and the future of energy.

This is his ninth book. His primary web site is https://davidhoule.com/

Made in the USA
Columbia, SC
27 June 2020

11059771R00070